PHONE SKILLS FOR THE INFORMATION AGE

THIRD EDITION

PHONE SKILLS FOR THE INFORMATION AGE

THIRD EDITION

DOROTHY MAXWELL

Boston   Burr Ridge, IL   Dubuque, IA   Madison, WI   New York   San Francisco   St. Louis
Bangkok   Bogotá   Caracas   Kuala Lumpur   Lisbon   London   Madrid   Mexico City
Milan   Montreal   New Delhi   Santiago   Seoul   Singapore   Sydney   Taipei   Toronto

McGraw-Hill
Irwin

PHONE SKILLS FOR THE INFORMATION AGE

Published by McGraw-Hill/Irwin, a business unit of The McGraw-Hill Companies, Inc., 1221 Avenue of the Americas, New York, NY, 10020. Copyright © 2006, 1998, 1991 by The McGraw-Hill Companies, Inc. All rights reserved. No part of this publication may be reproduced or distributed in any form or by any means, or stored in a database or retrieval system, without the prior written consent of The McGraw-Hill Companies, Inc., including, but not limited to, in any network or other electronic storage or transmission, or broadcast for distance learning.

Some ancillaries, including electronic and print components, may not be available to customers outside the United States.

This book is printed on acid-free paper.

1 2 3 4 5 6 7 8 9 0 QPD/QPD 0 9 8 7 6 5

ISBN 0-07-301727-2

Editorial director: *John E. Biernat*
Publisher: *Linda Schreiber*
Sponsoring editor: *Doug Hughes*
Developmental editor: *Megan Gates*
Editorial assistant: *Peter Vanaria*
Marketing manager: *Keari Bedford*
Media producer: *Benjamin Curless*
Project manager: *Harvey Yep*
Lead production supervisor: *Michael R. McCormick*
Design coordinator: *Cara David*
Photo research coordinator: *Kathy Shive*
Senior media project manager: *Rose M. Range*
Developer, Media technology: *Brian Nacik*
Cover design: *Cara David*
Cover images: *© Getty Images, © Corbis Images*
Interior design: *Cara David*
Typeface: *11.5/13 Times*
Compositor: *GTS – York, PA Campus*
Printer: *Quebecor World Dubuque Inc.*

Library of Congress Cataloging-in-Publication Data

Maxwell, Dorothy (Dorothy A.)
    Phone skills for the Information Age / Dorothy Maxwell.—3rd ed.
        p. cm.
    Includes index.
    ISBN 0-07-301727-2 (alk. paper)
    1. Phone in business. 2. Phone etiquette. I. Title.
HF5541.T4M39 2005
651.7′3—dc22

                                                                                              2004065601

www.mhhe.com

BRIEF CONTENTS

TABLE OF CONTENTS

CHAPTER 5
Servicing the Customer on the Phone 99

CHAPTER 6
Using Phone and Phone-Related Equipment and Technology 117

Dorothy A. Maxwell is a teacher of business and technology at Sacopee Valley High School in South Hiram, Maine, as well as Coordinator of Career and Technical Education and Teacher Induction. She has authored numerous articles and co-authored and authored several books in the area of business and education, including the two previous editions of this text-workbook.

Dorothy has been recognized by her colleagues and students by being named Maine's Teacher of the Year. She also has been recognized nationally by receiving a Milken Family Foundation National Educator Award and has served as President of the National Business Education Association. She currently serves on the Board of Directors for the Maine Association of Supervision and Curriculum Development as well as the York County Federal Credit Union.

Dorothy is a native of Maine and resides in Cornish, Maine, with her husband, Jim, and their two cats.

Dorothy may be reached at 207-625-4461 or by e-mail at djmaxwell@adelphia.net. Her mailing address is PO Box 646, Cornish, ME 04020-0646.

PHONE SKILLS FOR THE INFORMATION AGE, Third Edition, recognizes the extremely important role the phone plays in communicating globally in an efficient and professional manner.

Each of the six chapters in the text-workbook focuses on the following topics:

Chapter 1: Communicating Positively
Chapter 2: Making Phone Calls
Chapter 3: Handling Incoming Phone Calls
Chapter 4: Handling Special Types of Phone Calls
Chapter 5: Servicing the Customer on the Phone
Chapter 6: Using Phone and Phone-Related Equipment and Technology

Each chapter is supported by activities, pictures, and marginal reminders and concludes with a summary, reinforcement applications, and case studies to review and reinforce the emphasis of the topic being studied.

PHONE SKILLS FOR THE INFORMATION AGE, Third Edition, is supported by a DVD that reinforces concepts presented in the text-workbook. An Instructor's Resource CD contains teaching suggestions, PowerPoint presentations, and a test bank. Access to McGraw-Hill/Irwin's Online Learning Center provides additional support directly from the author as well as test questions.

By studying PHONE SKILLS FOR THE INFORMATION AGE, Third Edition, you will continue to learn and refine outstanding phone skills that you can use for a lifetime of positive communication!

—*Dorothy A. Maxwell*

DEDICATION

This book is dedicated to my husband, Dr. G.W. (Jim) Maxwell, a truly great communicator. Thank you for your love, inspiration, and support during the writing of PHONE SKILLS FOR THE INFORMATION AGE, Third Edition.

Communicating Positively

"The genius of communication is the ability to be both totally honest and totally kind at the same time."
—**John Powell**

Show
Power Point
slide

CHAPTER OBJECTIVES

Chapter 1 will help you:

1. Develop positive communication skills when using the phone.

2. Reinforce the importance LISTENING plays in the process of communicating.

3. Ask questions effectively.

4. Recognize the three major stages of a phone call and integrate them efficiently in the process of making a call.

5. Assess your phone skills and focus on areas for improvement.

You have been passed a note to respond immediately to a phone message. You step outside the room to an area where you can focus on returning the call using your cell phone or locating an available phone. Noise, distraction, and privacy are factors working against you in returning the call.

How would you handle this situation?

_____

_____

_____

_____

The truth of the matter is that every time you use a phone, whatever the type, you need to demonstrate positive communication skill. Your voice is you, and you always need to speak positively. You also need to listen actively in order to respond positively.

ASSESSMENT 1–1: ASSESS YOUR PHONE SKILLS

Directions: *Read the statement below and assess your phone skill by marking one of the three choices. Be as honest as you can.*

	Yes	Usually	Sometimes
1. I am in control of all calls I make.	____	____	____
2. I answer the phone using a friendly tone.	____	____	____
3. I have all necessary notes in front of me when I begin the call.	____	____	____
4. I ask appropriate questions.	____	____	____
5. My phone voice is pleasant.	____	____	____
6. I demonstrate positive listening skill.	____	____	____
7. I take accurate messages.	____	____	____
8. I am respectful of others when using the phone.	____	____	____
9. I am aware of time zone differences.	____	____	____
10. I use the most efficient phone technology for the situation.	____	____	____

Other comments concerning your phone

skills: _____

_____

_____

Phone skill on which I need to

focus: _____

_____

_____

Analysis: If you marked "Yes" to all statements, you have excellent phone
skills.

   If you marked "Yes" to all but one or two statements, you have very
good phone skills.

   If you marked "Yes" to fewer than five statements, you have several
areas you need to work on improving.

■ THE PROCESS OF COMMUNICATING

> **PICTURE THIS**
>
> You are faced with a situation requiring that you need immediate feedback from Margaret, a member of your team working on a time-sensitive project. When you phone Margaret, and she answers, you sense immediately by the tone of her voice that something is not quite right. You inquire whether this is a good time to speak with her, and she replies that she will get back to you shortly.

Discuss

> **ANALYZE THIS**
>
> What role does communication play in this situation?

_____

_____

Show second slide

What Is Communication?

Communication is the process of exchanging ideas and messages both verbally and/or nonverbally. Communication consists of ***four*** major parts: listening, reading, speaking, and writing—with ***listening*** being the most important part. Look at the graphic on the next page combining all four parts in a continuous circle of communication.

Show next slide

FIGURE 1.1 | The Four Segments of the Communication Process Interact

When you communicate via the phone, you are usually using all four parts of the communications process in some way. If a message is not received or conveyed in the manner that was intended, ***miscommunication*** occurs. Your major goal is to make the process of communication a natural habit, thus avoiding ***miscommunication.***

When you communicate via the phone, you have no visual images to guide you. Your ***listening*** skills are your guide. You listen to one or more speakers, depending on the type of call. Likewise the person or persons you are speaking with, depends on your voice and listening skills to prevent any miscommunication or confusion.

ACTIVITY 1-1

Communicating Without Seeing

Purpose: Understand the effect of communicating without seeing when you are using the phone.

Directions: *Select a partner for this activity. Turn your backs to each other, and have a short conversation about the best thing that has happened to each of you thus far today. After you have completed that conversation, turn around and face each other. Then, talk to each other about the worst thing that has happened to each of you today. After you have completed this activity, answer the following questions.*

1. Was it easier to communicate when you were back-to-back or face-to-face? Why?

    _____

    _____

    _____

    _____

    _____

2. What voice clues did you use to help you understand what your partner was saying when you had no visual contact?

_____

_____

_____

_____

_____

3. What visual clues did you use to help you understand what your partner was saying when you were face-to-face?

_____

_____

_____

_____

_____

4. What did you learn about communicating with no visual contact that will assist you when you are using the phone?

_____

_____

_____

_____

_____

Speaking

When you speak via the phone, your *voice* must do the job. A pleasant voice that is easy to listen to communicates a positive image and message.

Qualities of a Pleasant Voice!

Appropriate Volume—Not too loud or too soft. Change your volume to emphasize important information.

Comfortable Rate—Speak at a rate that allows your listener to absorb your message and take down notes either electronically or on paper.

Correct Pronunciation and Enunciation—*Pronunciation* is the correct way to say a word. *Enunciation* is the clarity with which you speak. Check the pronunciation of unfamiliar words electronically or with a traditional dictionary prior to using them. Enunciate words clearly as you speak.

ACTIVITY 1-2

Pronouncing and Enunciating

Purpose: Reinforce the importance of pronouncing and enunciating words correctly.

Directions: *Select a partner for this activity.*

Section 1
Read aloud the following list of words while your partner listens for correct pronunciation and enunciation of each word. Then reverse roles.

1. library
2. February
3. message
4. affect
5. comparable

6. compromise
7. laboratory
8. technical
9. experience
10. thorough

   After both of you have completed Section 1, assess your overall pronunciation and enunciation techniques noting areas of needed improvement.

Section 2
*List five words that you have difficulty **pronouncing** or **enunciating**. Use a dictionary to check the pronunciation of the words, if you are unsure. Practice saying each word aloud until you **pronounce** and **enunciate** it correctly.*

1. _____
2. _____
3. _____
4. _____
5. _____

Speaking Positively on the Phone

When you speak on the phone, the ***tone*** of your voice conveys your attitude or manner of expression. ***Pitch*** refers to the variation in tone of your voice. Vary the pitch of your voice to make the conversation interesting and pleasant.

Speaking Positively on the Phone

Stay Alert—Focus on the phone call. Pay attention to what you say and to what is being said to you. Be positioned physically in order to avoid as much distraction as possible.

Speak Directly into the Phone—Hold the phone an inch or two in front of your lips. Speak clearly and friendly, smiling as you speak. **Keep objects such as gum, food, and pens or pencils out of your mouth.**

Adjust Your Volume—Speak so that the listener can hear you. The quality of the phone connections can affect the listener's hearing level, requiring you to adjust your tone and pitch of voice.

Listen to Yourself—Certain factors can affect your voice. A cold may create a nasal sound in your voice. Stress may cause you to speak faster or slower. If you have an accent or dialect, speak slowly enough for the listener to understand.

FIGURE 1.2

Reading and Writing

Writing, reading, and interpreting phone messages is an extremely important skill in the process of phone communication. You should ALWAYS be prepared to record messages and any other information when using the phone. Write messages clearly in a style so that they can be read quickly and responded to appropriately. (Reading, writing, and interpreting messages will be covered in greater detail in a later chapter.)

Listening

As noted earlier in this chapter, when you are using the phone, *listening* is the most important part of communicating. The saying "many hear but few listen" accurately describes what often happens when people are using the phone. Listening combines both physical and mental skill and implies understanding by responding in an appropriate manner.

> *Listening* involves four related steps: ***sensing, interpreting, evaluating***, and ***responding***. (See Figure 1.3.)

> *Sensing* indicates your awareness that something is being said to which you need to listen. Without sensing a need for listening, the process does not occur.

> *Interpreting* is identifying what is said and explaining the speaker's meaning. While you may hear the words, if you do not understand what the speaker intended, it is very easy to misinterpret a message. Your personal interest, knowledge, experience, and personality are all influential factors in how well you interpret what you hear.

> *Evaluating* requires you to think about the entire message and conclude about its content as well as the way you will respond.

> *Responding* indicates that you need to make a verbal statement.

FIGURE 1.3 | Accurate listening is based on the four related steps of the listening process.

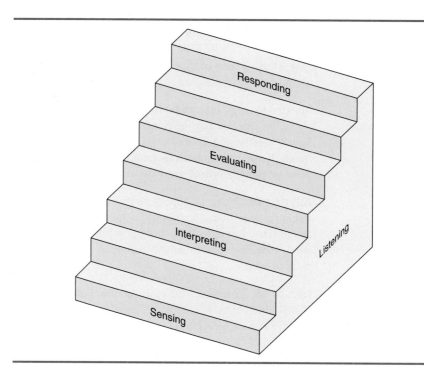

ASSESSMENT 1–2: ASSESS YOUR LISTENING SKILL

Directions: *Read the statements and assess your listening skill by marking one of the four choices. Be as honest as you can.*

	Always	Sometimes	Seldom	Needs Improvement
1. I listen for facts.	____	____	____	____
2. I concentrate on main ideas.	____	____	____	____
3. I give appropriate feedback.	____	____	____	____
4. I am prepared to listen when I am using the phone.	____	____	____	____
5. I take notes.	____	____	____	____
6. I avoid distractions.	____	____	____	____
7. I ask questions when necessary.	____	____	____	____
8. I avoid making premature conclusions.	____	____	____	____
9. I avoid interrupting the person to whom I am speaking.	____	____	____	____
10. I practice phone courtesy.	____	____	____	____

Overall assessment of my Listening

Skill: _____

_____

_____

Areas on which I need to

focus: _____

_____

_____

Analysis: If you marked "Yes" to all statements, you have excellent listening skill.

If you marked "Yes" to all but one or two statements, you have very good listening skill.

If you marked "Yes" to less than five statements, you have several areas you need to work on improving.

Active Listening—What Does It Mean?

Active listening as it relates to using a phone means that you MUST hear words and thoughts and respond to them. Why do people not listen actively when they are using the phone? Perhaps their interest or knowledge level is limited.

Improving your listening skill will help you gain confidence whenever you are using the phone—whatever the situation. Improved listening skill can result in improved work performance. Always attempt to keep a positive attitude when using the phone, recognizing the reality that everything you hear may not be positive.

When you are making or answering a phone call, be ready to LISTEN. While the buzz, beep, or ring of the phone may distract you before you answer the phone, focus your thoughts on the conversation when you pick up the call.

ACTIVITY 1-3

Positive and Negative Phone Talk

Purpose: Evaluate phone comments as being positive or negative.

Directions: *Place a check mark in the* **Positive** *column if you think the comment is positive, or in the* **Negative** *column if you think it is negative. Be prepared to justify your answers. If possible, read these comments aloud with a partner. Notice how using different tones of voice positively and negatively affect listening when you are using the phone.*

	Positive	Negative
1. "When will you make a decision about whether you will go to the conference? Don't you think it is about time you did?"	_____	_____
2. "The Advertising Department must have quoted you the wrong price. Hold on, I'll transfer you."	_____	_____
3. "Our records show that your balance is $5329.10. When do you plan to make a payment or let us know how you plan to pay the balance?"	_____	_____
4. "It will be a pleasure to speak at the meeting in Omaha on March 23. I'm thrilled you invited me."	_____	_____
5. "Please don't shout at us. We were not responsible for that decision."	_____	_____
6. "I absolutely will not do as you requested. That is a ridiculous idea."	_____	_____
7. "Why doesn't someone speak to her about her constant habit of interrupting whenever someone else is speaking?"	_____	_____
8. "Thank you for calling. I am glad we could be of service to you."	_____	_____
9. "He never listens to anything anyone tells him. He is so headstrong. This could be disastrous for him at performance review time."	_____	_____
10. "Would you explain the situation to me, please?"	_____	_____

Listening Roadblocks

It is likely that you may encounter listening roadblocks such as *distractions*, *interruptions,* or *disconnected* calls. These roadblocks often occur unexpectedly. You need to be ready to handle whatever roadblocks occur.

Dealing with Distractions   Distractions are almost impossible to avoid. Some activity and sounds will be loud or unusual. Other sounds will blend into the background. Still other distracting sounds may come from the phone if the connection is poor.

How do you handle distractions? You could ask people to be quiet. If movement or activity is bothering you, try turning your back to it or looking down at your desk rather than around the office. This will help you concentrate on the conversation. If your call requires privacy, locate an area that provides it—you may even have to return the call. If the phone connection continues to interfere with your conversation, explain this to the other person and offer to call back.

Handling Interruptions   Interruptions are among the most annoying interferences when using a phone. If someone tries to speak with you while you are on the phone, use a signal that indicates you are unavailable at the moment. Put a finger to your lips to indicate "silence please," or raise your hand in a stop signal. If this does not work, excuse yourself from the call and tell the interrupter that you are in the middle of a call and will have to speak with them later. When you return to the person on the phone, thank them for waiting.

ACTIVITY 1-4

Interference with Listening When Using the Phone

Purpose: Analyze your listening skills as they relate to interference when using the phone.

Directions: *Place a check mark beside any of the items below that interfere with your listening when using the phone.*

_____   **1.** Noise can be heard on the phone line.

_____   **2.** The caller does not respond or acknowledge comments,

_____   **3.** The person being called keeps repeating the same message.

_____   **4.** The speaker is giving information that is too involved for phone discussion.

_____   **5.** The speaker does not speak clearly and is mumbling words.

_____   **6.** The party being called speaks either too loudly or too softly.

_____   **7.** The party being called is using vocabulary that is difficult to understand.

_____   **8.** The caller thinks you already know the purpose of the call.

_____   **9.** You can hear a lot of background interference such as talking or music.

_____   **10.** You are aware that the person with whom you are talking is simultaneously having another conversation with someone else.

Disconnected Calls   Disconnected calls occur as a result of power failure, overloaded lines, storms, or accidental pressing of buttons. If you are disconnected on a call, place the call again. If you disconnect a call from someone whose number you do not know, wait for that party to return the call to you. If the cause of the disconnection is unclear, then normally the party who initiated the call should call again. When you call back, simply say, "I'm sorry, we got disconnected somehow."

ACTIVITY 1-5

Dealing with Distractions

Purpose: Learn options for dealing with distractions.

Directions: *Read each scenario below and respond to the questions.*

Scenario: *Cindy works in a busy office area with seven other team members. Team members walk around her desk talking frequently, even when Cindy is on the phone. Even worse, one of her team members plays a radio that is tuned to a talk show. Of course, Cindy has a very difficult time concentrating.*

1. What can Cindy do about the level of noise and activity taking place around her desk?

_____

_____

_____

_____

_____

_____

_____

_____

2. How should Cindy handle the person who plays the radio?

_____

_____

_____

_____

_____

_____

_____

_____

3. What actions can Cindy take to improve her concentration when she is using the phone?

_____

_____

_____

_____

_____

_____

_____

_____

_____

Overcoming Listening Roadblocks

1. When you make a call, find a place where there will be no loud voices or other loud interference. If an interference occurs during a call, excuse yourself from the phone conversation; then ask the other people to be quiet. In extreme situations, find another phone to use.

2. Keep your emotions in check. Remain objective at all times and be aware of certain situations, words, or individuals that tend to trigger emotions when you are using the phone.

3. Ask meaningful questions. (Questioning will be covered in detail later in Chapter 1).

4. Practice patience and courtesy at all times. A pause in the phone conversation does not mean a breakdown has occurred in the discussion. Clarification may be needed.

5. Be prepared to actively listen whenever you pick up the phone.

6. Listen for specific information. Irrelevant information can cause you to forget the main part of the message.

7. Ask for information to be repeated if you did not understand it.

8. Use the information as soon as possible or record the information for later reference.

9. Use interjections throughout the phone conversation. By saying "I understand" or "yes," you are demonstrating to the other party that you are listening.

10. Practice listening with coworkers, friends, and relatives. If you practice good listening skills, you can improve them.

Listening Techniques for Improved Phone Skill

Be ready to listen.   Focus on the speaker and the situation. If you are daydreaming or trying to do something else while speaking on the phone, you are not ready to listen. Keep note-taking supplies handy.

Concentrate.   Distractions interfere with the listening process. If you are thinking of other things you have to do, it is easy to lose concentration on what is being said to you or what you are saying over the phone.

Speak directly into the mouthpiece of the phone (or appropriate device if you are involved in a conference call).   Use a pleasant voice and clear pronunciation and enunciation.

Be enthusiastic.   This conveys a positive image of both you and the business you represent.

Listen for details and key words.   By listening for details and key words, you will be able to comprehend the message faster and better.

Ask questions when necessary.   If the situation calls for a response, be ready to ask questions when the opportunity arises. Allow the speaker to finish a statement, and then ask the question. Repeat the speaker's ideas in your own words to make it easier for you to remember what was said.

■ STAGES OF A PHONE CALL

The saying "You never get a second chance to make a good first impression" is especially true when it comes to using the phone. Whether you are making or receiving a call, practicing good phone skills allows you to make a great "first impression."

Courtesy and *professionalism* are the bench marks of positive phone skills. When you are courteous, you are considerate of the people with whom you are communicating. When you are professional, you communicate in a way that creates a sense of satisfaction for both parties.

Every phone call you make can be compared to a play in which you are a major actor. It would be wonderful if all play performances were outstanding, but some performances are better than others. Likewise, you are always on stage to complete a phone call courteously and professionally.

Phone calls can be divided into three stages: the **introduction,** the **purpose,** and the **conclusion.** All three stages are equally important to a successful call.

Attitude is everything on the telephone—keep a good one!

The Introduction

Whether you are making or answering a call, the first few seconds of the call are very important. During this *introduction* phase, the parties should be identified and the convenience of the call established. These phone courtesies should ALWAYS be observed!

Identifying Yourself and the Other Party   Answer the phone promptly, at least by the second ring, identifying yourself pleasantly. See the examples that follow:

FIGURE 1.4

When you answer your own phone, say:
"Jessica Vergaard speaking."

When you answer a department phone, say:
"Customer Service; this is Clyde Wolczyk."

When you answer for a firm, say:
"Good morning, Commissioner's office. This is Sunitha speaking."

When you answer another person's phone, say:
"Dr. Brown's office; this is Brenda."

When you make a call and the other party answers the phone with a greeting and an identification, immediately identify yourself and your employer, if appropriate.

Caller: "Hello, this is Anna Dearborn from the Cornish Chamber of Commerce."

Recipient: "Hello, Ms. Dearborn. This is Sophia Davis."

If the other person does not identify himself or herself, or if you did not hear the name clearly, courteously ask the name.

"May I have your name, please?"

"Excuse me. Would you please spell your last name?"

"I would be happy to help you. May I ask who is calling?"

If it is necessary to put the caller on "hold," periodically ask the caller if he or she wishes to continue "holding" or to leave a message. If the person being called is unavailable, take a message instead of keeping the caller on hold. (Taking messages will be covered in Chapter 3.) Nothing can ruin customer satisfaction or credibility more than being placed on "hold" for long periods of time. A call might be similar to the following:

Caller: "May I speak with Ms. Parker?"

Recipient: "Please hold; I'll check if she is in her office." (*pause*)
"Ms. Parker is not available at this time. Could I take a message?"

Establishing the Convenience of the Call   When you make a phone call, you have no idea what the recipient was doing prior to your call. Your call may interrupt an important activity. Therefore, unless your call is an emergency, make sure that the recipient has time to talk with you. Establish the convenience of the call, particularly if it is an international call or a long-distance call involving different time zones. For example, you might say:

) "Is this a convenient time for us to speak?"

⌐ "May I have a few moments of your time?"

Using these phrases gives the person receiving the call a chance to reply politely whether it is a convenient time to speak.

What do you do if someone calls you, interrupting an important task that you cannot set aside, and immediately launches into the business of the call? If this happens, wait for the person to pause. Indicate that the immediate moment is inconvenient for you to talk and offer to return the call.

) "Could I call you back in a few minutes, Courtney? I need to finish the project I am working on."

⌐ "Mr. Alawi, I have a meeting to attend. May I call you back this afternoon?"

ACTIVITY 1-6

Courteous and Professional Communication

Purpose: Develop an awareness for courteous and professional procedure at the beginning of a phone call.

Directions: *Read each statement and determine if it is courteous and professional. If it is, place a check mark in the* **Yes** *column. If it is not, place a check mark in the* **No** *column; then rewrite the statement to make it courteous and professional.*

	Yes	No
1. **Caller (Mr. Worton)** "Is Elizabeth Waters there?"		✓
2. **Caller (Judy Wright, Human Resources):** "Hello, Mr. Lyons. This is Judy Wright from Human Resources."	✓	
3. **Receiver (Jane Stevens, Customer Service):** "Customer Service."		✓
4. **Receiver (John Spisak, Shipping and Receiving):** "I can't talk now. I'm in the middle of something more important."		✓

5. **Caller (Louise Stone):** "Good morning. May I ask who this is?"

_____   _____

_____

_____

_____

6. **Receiver (Darrell Chin):** "Who is this? I can't hear you."

_____   ✓_____

_____

_____

_____

Next slide

The Purpose

After you have exchanged introductory courtesies, establish the **purpose** of the call. One person needs something from the other; otherwise, the call would not have been made. During this stage of the call, communicate your needs clearly and make sure you understand the other person's needs as well. Do this by expressing your needs, asking questions, and confirming what you are hearing.

Expressing Your Needs   Usually the person placing the call is the one who wants something. That person should state the problem or request clearly and politely, and then give the other party a chance to respond. For example:

"Could you tell me the colors and sizes these shirts come in? I lost my catalog."

"Would it be possible for me to set up an appointment to speak with Mr. Hinds concerning the textbook account?"

"We are having a problem with our copier and would like to have it serviced as soon as possible."

Express what you want in a firm, courteous manner. Avoid being rude, negative, or submissive.

Rudeness: "This stupid copier is broken again!"

Negative: "I'm not putting up with this!"

Submissiveness: "I'm sorry to have to bother you, but I think we've done something wrong with the copier; it's just not working right."

ACTIVITY 1-7

Expressing Needs over the Phone

Purpose: Practice expressing your needs as directly as possible when you are using the phone.

Do

Directions: *Read each following statement and write a statement to express your needs in a courteous and professional manner.*

1. You want to order five boxes of computer paper. The boxes MUST be delivered within two days.

_____

_____

_____

2. You ordered seven boxes of staples, but received seven boxes of paper clips.

_____

_____

_____

3. You need to see Jean Simard for approximately one hour within the next two days.

_____

_____

_____

4. You have tried unsuccessfully to reach Mr. Callahan on the phone for three days. You need to see him sometime today in order to finalize a project before the deadline.

_____

_____

_____

5. Because of an emergency, you are calling to reschedule an appointment.

_____

_____

_____

Open questions
require more of an answer
than *yes* or *no* and usually
begin with *who, what,
where, when, why,* and *how.*

Closed questions
can be answered with *yes* or
no and often start with *are
you, do you, can, could, did,
will,* and *would.*

Questioning Over the Phone   Ask questions to obtain information. The information may help you answer the other party's request or clarify a response to your needs. Creative questions will yield positive results. Three basic types of questions help you obtain information.

Open Questions   Open questions require more than a *yes* or *no* answer; for example:

"How may I assist you?"

"What date is convenient for us to meet for lunch?"

"What seems to be the problem with the printer?"

These questions require more information and detail. Open questions usually begin with *who, what, where, when, why,* and *how.*

Closed Questions   Closed questions can be answered with a *yes* or *no* answer. For example:

"Would you like to order the blue labels?"

"Will you be available at 4 p.m. on Friday?"

"Is the machine transmitting?"

Closed questions are used to verify information. They often start with the words *are you, do you, can, could, did, will,* and *would.*

Feedback questions require an *either-or* response.

Formulate your questions carefully in order to obtain pertinent information.

Feedback Questions Feedback questions require response. You give the listener a choice of two or more options from which to select. For example:

"Would you prefer us to meet you at The Lobster Pot Restaurant at 12:30 p.m. or 12:45 p.m. for lunch?"

"Would you care to place your order today or tomorrow?"

ACTIVITY 1-8

Identifying Questions over the Phone

Purpose: Identify the three major types of questions and develop an awareness for using a particular type of question when using the phone.

Directions: *Identify each question as* open, closed, *or* feedback. *Know why you made your choice.*

<u>O</u> **1.** What did you do with the phone number I gave you?

<u>C</u> **2.** Have you paid for the tickets to the concert?

<u>F</u> **3.** Should I send the final check to the old address or the new address?

<u>O</u> **4.** For what type of position are you interested in applying?

<u>O</u> **5.** Why do you think the supplier will miss the delivery date?

<u>C</u> **6.** Do you plan to tour the new plant when you are in Boston?

<u>C</u> **7.** Those were very high standards, weren't they?

<u>O</u> **8.** Why wasn't it possible to record that information?

<u>C</u> **9.** Can it be repaired within two days?

<u>F</u> **10.** Would you prefer to purchase $100,000 or $150,000 worth of coverage?

<u>C</u> **11.** Did your supervisor tell you the whole story?

<u>F</u> **12.** How many calls did we log yesterday?

Suggestions for Positive Questioning

Listen attentively to all questions. Use those questions to rephrase your own questions to get the result you desire.

Pay attention to how questions are phrased and the words used to begin the question. This helps you focus more closely on the answer you may give.

Jot down the major questions you want to ask before you begin. You will feel more confident and in control of the questions during the phone call.

> **Confirm what you hear by asking questions that verify the information.**   Summarizing the confirmation will help you verify additional information.
>
> **Create a comfortable feeling between you and the other party by asking questions in a pleasant manner.**   Avoid tension and edginess. Smile when you are asking questions. It loosens your vocal chords for easier speaking.

The Conclusion

In the *conclusion* stage of a phone call, the caller and receiver come to an understanding of the action to be taken by each of them. Then they say good-bye.

Understanding the Action to Be Taken   If you are the one who is going to take action, verify what you are going to do or what will happen.

> "I'll see that Ms. Schneider gets your message as soon as she returns."
>
> "Your order will be processed and you should receive the merchandise within ten business days."
>
> "I will check on the status of your claim and get back to you within a day."

If you are unsure of anything that has been agreed upon during the call, confirm your information by asking closed questions.

> "Will you be out of the office this afternoon?"
>
> "Do you wish to order the office supplies at this time?"
>
> "Is the policy issued in both you and your husband's name?"

Summarizing a phone call can help avoid miscommunications later.

If a lot of information has been exchanged during the call, it is helpful to summarize what has been said. This brings closure to the call and reviews the call and the action needed.

Closing the Phone Call   Once the two parties understand the action to be taken, they can end the call. Sometimes you must take the initiative to end a call if the other party continues to talk after the business has been conducted. You can do this courteously by saying a statement such as:

> "I appreciate your calling, Mr. Chin."
>
> "It was nice to speak with you today, Jim. Thanks for calling and updating me on the status of the revision."

Statements like these show interest in the other party and also communicate that you are ready to end the call.

End the phone call pleasantly and professionally, avoiding colloquial expressions and slang.

You should always end the call by saying "good-bye" in a pleasant tone of voice. Avoid colloquial expressions (such as "talk to you later," "bye-bye," "see yah") that do not project a professional image.

After you say good-bye, allow the other party to hang up first. This ensures that you do not cut the other person off too quickly. Then place the receiver gently on its cradle or press the appropriate button to terminate the call.

FIGURE 1.5

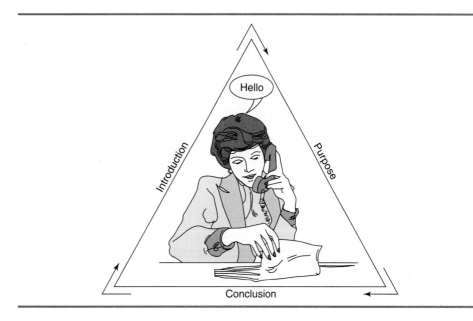

SUMMARY

1. As technology advances, the phone continues to be an important communication tool.

2. Learning how to refine your phone skills can improve communication and goodwill both personally and professionally.

3. Communication is the process of exchanging ideas and messages either verbally or nonverbally. Communication consists of four major parts: speaking, reading, writing, and listening—with listening being one of the most important.

4. Communicating on the phone differs from communicating face-to-face: you cannot see the other person or party.

5. When you speak on the phone, you cannot use your appearance, posture, eye contact, and gestures to help convey your message. Your voice must do the job.

6. Vary the pitch of your voice in order to make it interesting and pleasant to hear.

7. You must learn to read and interpret phone messages successfully.

8. Listening involves four related steps: sensing, interpreting, evaluating, and responding.

9. When you use the phone to communicate, you must practice active listening. Active listening means that you hear words and thoughts and need to respond to them.

10. When you pick up the phone receiver, be ready to listen.

11. To deal with the roadblocks of distractions, interruptions, and disconnected calls when using the phone, prepare for and know how to manage them.

12. Whenever you are using the phone, keep in mind that *courtesy* and *professionalism* are the bench marks of positive telephone skills.

13. Whether you are making or answering a call, the first few seconds of the call are very important.

14. If it is necessary to put the caller on "hold," periodically ask the caller if he or she wishes to continue "holding" or to leave a message.

15. Establish the convenience of the call, particularly if it is an international call or a long-distance call involving different time zones.

16. Ask questions to obtain information you need in order to answer the other party's request or to clarify a response to your needs.

17. In the conclusion stage of a phone call, the caller and receiver come to an understanding of the action to be taken by each of them and then say good-bye.

▉ APPLICATION ACTIVITY 1–1

Listening for Positive Communication

Directions: *Select a partner to work with you on this speaking and listening activity. Designate one person as Partner A and the other as Partner B. Partner A should read the following statement to Partner B. Partner B should be able to hear but not see Partner A, and should be prepared to take notes. This activity is to simulate a phone conversation between two people.*

Script for Partner A   Hello, this is Courtney Eastman, Administrator of Customer Services. Please make your cashiers aware of a major problem McKenney Foods has been having with bad checks. On Thursday, June 1, a customer successfully passed a bad check in the amount of $178.35 at the North Baldwin store. The customer was using the name June Rostberg, spelled R-O-S-T-B-E-R-G. On Saturday, June 3, another bad check for $91.21 was passed at the Cornish store by a person using the name of Jan Roastberg, spelled R-O-A-S-T-B-E-R-G. On the following Tuesday, June 6, a person using the name of Jane Roseburg (R-O-S-E-B-U-R-G) passed another bad check for $158.10, again at the Cornish store. In all cases, the customer showed a form of identification that the cashier accepted. Please emphasize to your cashiers that only proper identification (driver's license or McKenney Foods check-cashing ID card) is acceptable and should be checked carefully. Thank you for your prompt attention to this matter.

Partner B should now answer the following questions:

1. Who was the caller?

   _____

2. How many bad checks were passed?

   _____

3. What were the names used by the customer?

   _____

4. What identification should the cashiers accept from customers wanting to pay by check?

   _____

   _____

5. What qualities of Partner A's voice helped you listen to and understand this statement?

   _____

   _____

6. What could Partner A have done to improve voice tone and speaking techniques?

   _____

   _____

7. What could you have done to improve your listening skill?

_____

_____

▌ APPLICATION ACTIVITY 1–2

Do You Have a Minute to Answer My Questions?

Scenario: *Visualize that you are Margarita Hoxell who operates a graphic arts business in your home. A short time ago you responded to an online survey concerning types and styles of paper that you use in your business. You have just picked up on a phone call connected with the completed online survey asking you a few questions. You agree to answer them as long as it doesn't take more than a few minutes.*

Directions: *As the questions are asked, identify the types of questions and how they relate to the total phone conversation. At the end of the conversation, assess the questioning and reflect on the effectiveness of the call.*

	Type of Question
Question 1	
Ms. Hoxell, what types of paper do you use in your business?	_____
Question 2	
Is your color preference white or ivory?	_____
Question 3	
How would you like the heading formatted?	_____
Question 4	
Would you care to order the stationery today?	_____
Question 5	
Would you like to have your name included on our online newsletter?	_____

Analysis:

1. In your opinion, were the questions worded in a constructive style to yield the needed information?

_____

_____

2. How do you feel about your own skill in asking questions while using the phone?

_____

_____

CASE STUDY 1.1

The Interrupting Manager

Directions: *Analyze the situation described below and then answer the questions that follow.*

Kelley is the administrative assistant to three managers in the graphic arts department of a large printing and desktop publishing firm. A major problem has been occurring: numerous thoughtless interruptions are occurring when people are using the phone, due mainly to the staff's many pending deadlines. At a recent staff meeting, the situation was discussed, and everyone agreed to make an effort to be more courteous to people who are on the phone.

Two of Kelley's managers have been very conscientious about not interrupting. This improvement has definitely made her work easier. However, the third manager has made no attempt to improve his interruptions. He walks up to Kelley's desk at will and starts to give her directions about a task while she is on the phone. He has a loud voice, which makes it difficult for Kelley to hear the person on the other end of the phone. Kelley has been forced to ask customers to hold at least three times in the last two days in order to listen to the demands of her uncooperative manager.

This situation is very embarrassing. In fact, one potential customer became very upset and hung up after holding for several minutes, even though Kelley returned to speaking to the potential customer approximately every twenty seconds.

1. How is Kelley trying to handle the problem of her managers' interruptions?

   _____

   _____

   _____

   _____

2. Do you think the fact that the third manager is one of her bosses is affecting Kelley's handling of the situation? Why or why not?

   _____

   _____

   _____

   _____

3. What steps can Kelley take to try to change the third manager's behavior?

   _____

   _____

   _____

   _____

4. How do the four major components of communication (speaking, reading, writing, and listening) affect the situation with which Kelley is faced?

_____

_____

_____

_____

CASE STUDY 1.2

Receptionist in a Communication Crisis!

Directions: *Analyze the situation described below and then answer the questions that follow.*

A situation has developed with Esther, the new receptionist, in the office of a busy law firm where you work. You are the administrative assistant to one of the major partners in the business. It seems that the new receptionist is not using the script provided to clearly communicate with callers. She is often chewing gum or candy and is not listening attentively to phone callers. She often uses incorrect English and mispronounces the name of the law firm. Her questioning skills often do not yield a favorable reply and cause major miscommunication and confusion. She came highly recommended, but this is ridiculous. The situation is growing worse by the day.

1. How is Esther's lack of positive communication on the phone affecting the operation of the law firm?

_____

_____

_____

2. What steps would you recommend be taken to improve Esther's phone skills?

_____

_____

_____

3. Have you encountered any situations similar to these? Briefly explain.

_____

_____

_____

Making Phone Calls

"If it takes a lot of words to say what you have in mind, give it more thought."
—Dennis Roth

CHAPTER OBJECTIVES

Chapter 2 will help you:

1. Recognize the importance of planning before making a phone call.

2. Improve your phone attitude when making a phone call.

3. Use reference tools efficiently when making a phone call.

4. Recognize the types of phone calls and the best use of each.

5. Become familiar with the types of services that service providers offer.

PICTURE THIS

You consider yourself to be a pretty efficient person when it comes to using a phone. In fact, you recently purchased a new cell phone to help you even more. On this particular morning, you are making calls to follow up a potential sale of a new piece of office equipment. Suddenly, you realize that you have not saved the number electronically. Time is short. What should you do?

_____

_____

_____

Phones are an integral part of the process of communication in today's fast-paced world. You can purchase a phone with a wide variety of services to assist you in making calls efficiently, which can save you time and money both personally and professionally.

ASSESSMENT 2–1: ASSESS YOUR PHONE READINESS

Directions: *Read the statement below and assess your phone readiness by marking one of three choices. Be as honest as you can.*

	Yes	Usually	Sometimes
1. I think positively before I begin the call.	_____	_____	_____
2. I know the REASON I am making the call.	_____	_____	_____
3. I have all the necessary information in front of me before I make the call.	_____	_____	_____
4. I schedule the call at a convenient time.	_____	_____	_____
5. I have the correct number and have used a current phone directory or electronic directory if necessary.	_____	_____	_____
6. I am utilizing available phone services that are cost efficient and meet my needs.	_____	_____	_____

7. I am aware of and practice efficient phone safety and security at all times.   ____   ____   ____

8. I try to be aware of time zones when making calls.   ____   ____   ____

Analysis: If you marked "Yes" to all statements, your phone readiness is excellent.

If you marked "Yes" to all but one or two statements, you have very good phone readiness.

If you marked "Yes" to fewer than five statements, you have several areas you need to work on improving in the area of phone readiness.

■ PREPARING TO MAKE PHONE CALLS

Remember to smile as you speak on the phone. This is an important positive phone skill.

next slide

You need to be ready mentally and physically before you make any phone call by demonstrating a positive attitude. Be certain that you know the PURPOSE of your call. Typically, you are calling for one or more of the following reasons:

- Providing or confirming information.
- Returning a phone call.
- Solving a problem.

As the call progresses, anticipate potential conversations that may develop. Be prepared with as much of the necessary materials as possible BEFORE you make the call. This might include such information as account numbers, catalogs, or other related identifying material. If applicable to the situation, having a computer readily available where you can easily access information can be very helpful.

Depending on the situation, you may have to make calls on behalf of others. When this is the case, the same procedure applies, except that you are speaking for another person.

Whatever the situation, PLAN for the call and follow these basic steps:

next slide
1. Identify yourself immediately and greet the person. Inquire whether this is a good time to speak with the party called. This gets the call off on a positive note.

   "Hello, Cindy, this is Heidi. Is this a good time to speak with you?"

next slide
2. Tell the person WHY you are calling. Choose your words wisely.

   "I'm calling about setting a time for your interview."

next slide
3. Ask questions so that both of you understand the call, and determine the action needed.

   "It sounds as if Thursday afternoon would be the best time for you, is that correct?"

next slide
4. Close the call in a friendly manner. Be sure that both parties understand the outcome to reach as the result of the call.

   "I'll look forward to seeing you at 2:30 on Thursday afternoon, Good-bye."

For example, assume that you are making airline reservations. You will need to have the following information before making the call:

FIGURE 2.1

International Calling Codes

	Time Difference		*Time Difference*		*Time Difference*
Algeria *213	+6	**China 86**	+13	Guatemala City 2	
American Samoa *684	−6	Beijing (Peking)1		**Guyana 592**	+2
Argentina 54	+2	Guangzhou (Canton) 20		**Haiti 509**	0
Buenos Aires 1		Shanghai 21		Port au Prince 1	
Aruba 297	+1	**Colombia 57**	0	**Honduras* 504**	−1
Australia 61	+15	Bogota 1		**Hong Kong** 852**	+13
Melbourne 3		**Costa Rica* 506**	−1	**Hungary 36**	+6
Sydney 2		**Cyprus 357**	+7	Budapest 1	
Austria 43	+6	**Czech Republic 42**	+6	**Iceland 354**	+5
Vienna 1		Prague 2		Reykjavik 1	
Bahrain* 973	+8	**Denmark 45**	+6	**India 91**	+10½
Bangladesh 880	+11	Copenhagen 1 or 2		Bombay 22	
Belgium 32	+6	**Ecuador 593**	0	Calcutta 33	
Antwerp 3		Guayaquil 4		New Delhi 11	
Brussels 2		Quito 2		**Indonesia 62**	+12
Belize 501	−1	**Egypt 20**	+7	Jakarta 21	
Bolivia 591	+1	Alexandria 3		**Iran 98**	+8½
La Paz 2		Cairo 2		Teheran 21	
Brazil 55	+2	**El Salvador* 503**	−1	**Iraq 964**	+8
Brasilia 61		**Ethiopia 251**	+8	Baghdad 1	
Rio de Janeiro 21		Addis Ababa 1		**Ireland 353**	+5
Sao Paulo 11		**Fiji* 679**	+17	Dublin 1	
Cameroon* 237	+6	**Finland 358**	+7	**Israel 972**	+7
Chile 56	+1	Helsinki 0		Jerusalem 2	
Santiago 2	+13	**Guatemala 502**	−1	Tel Aviv 3	

What are the departure and return dates?

Do you have an airline preference?

Do you require any special services?

As you make the reservation, ask questions such as the following:

Are the tickets refundable?

Could you review the complete itinerary with me?

What forms of identification do I need?

Are there any restrictions I need to know?

In order to make a successful airline reservation, all of this information is essential. As the call continues, you might think of additional questions. Have materials for taking notes handy and, if applicable, access to a computer to assist you in completing your call.

Scheduling Your Phone Call

When you are making a call, you are in control of your readiness for the call. If the call you need to make involves calling a different time zone, you need to be certain that you are familiar with the hours a business you might be calling is open. If it is an individual, you still need to be sensitive to the time factor. Refer to the time zone map in your local phone directory, or use the Internet to verify the time difference between where you are and where you are calling. If necessary, check the international country and city codes in your phone directory. Some directories list the time difference from a specific time zone to other countries. Whatever the situation, consider carefully WHERE you are calling when you are calling outside of your time zone.

ACTIVITY 2-1

Making Long-Distance Calls in a "Timely" Manner

Purpose: To help you analyze the appropriate time to make long-distance, domestic, and international calls.

Directions: *Assume that it is 9 A.M. in your office in Boston, Massachusetts. You have several calls to make to branch offices of your company located both in the United States and other countries. You know that the office hours at all locations are from 9 A.M. to 5 P.M. Monday through Friday.*

Refer to the time zone chart in your local phone directory. Then, write the local time next to each item below. Place a check mark by Call Now *or* Do Not Call Now *according to whether it would be appropriate to call at 9 A.M. Boston time.*

	Time	Call Now	Do Not Call Now
1. Los Angeles, California	——	——	——
2. Miami, Florida	——	——	——
3. Dallas, Texas	——	——	——
4. Chicago, Illinois	——	——	——
5. Seattle, Washington	——	——	——
6. Amsterdam, The Netherlands	——	——	——
7. Stockholm, Sweden	——	——	——
8. Cape Town, South Africa	——	——	——
9. Geneva, Switzerland	——	——	——
10. London, United Kingdom	——	——	——

Locating the Correct Phone Number

To save both time and money, make sure that you have the correct phone number BEFORE you begin the call. You can locate phone numbers by using personal directories, company directories, phone directories both locally and otherwise (which include Yellow Pages), and electronic directories that you may have organized or that you may use the Internet to find the correct number. Most Internet browsers have a *White Pages* and *Yellow Pages* tab that you can click on to activate an electronic phone directory. Beware of websites that offer advanced searching, as you may be charged an additional fee.

If you are using a cell phone, you can store numbers electronically.

If you absolutely cannot locate a phone number using one of the approaches mentioned above, call *directory assistance.* You should be aware that many service providers have restrictions on the number of times you can use directory assistance without charging a fee.

Be certain that you use the telephone number, not the fax number, when making a call.

Directory assistance, or Information, can help you locate local or long-distance telephone numbers.

■ PHONE DIRECTORIES

Using the White Pages

The **White Pages** of a phone directory provide an alphabetic listing of names and other phone reference information. The front pages of the phone directory contain a wide range of information related to using the phone.

FIGURE 2.2 | Residential and government office listings from a White Pages directory.

The next section of the phone directory typically contains the ***residence listings***.

The next section contains ***business listings*** of local businesses and/or organizations.

Some local directories contain listings of local, state, and federal government offices and agencies. These listings might be incorporated into the business listing section, or they may be in a separate section of the phone book. These government listings typically are arranged by the name of the state government (such as *Maine, State of*) and then by departments or agencies. See Figure 2-2 for examples of government listings.

The Yellow Pages

The *Yellow Pages* is a directory of listings or display ads for organizations and businesses. The listings and ads are arranged alphabetically by subject heading. Often they are cross-referenced under related subjects. The *Yellow Pages* can appear within the phone directory, or it may be published separately. (See Figure 2-3 for a sample of business listings.)

Use the *Yellow Pages* when you need to locate a product or service. For example, if you need information about purchasing a new computer, look for the heading "computers." This listing will contain several businesses from

FIGURE 2.3 | Listings from a Yellow Pages directory.

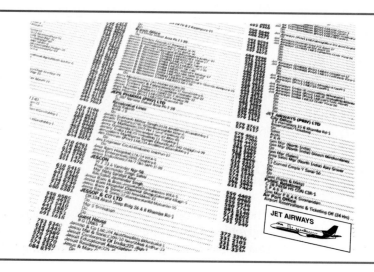

which to select. If you cannot locate information on a particular topic in the *Yellow Pages,* search under related headings or subjects.

ACTIVITY 2-2

"Let Your Fingers Do the Walking"

Purpose: Practice locating information in the *Yellow Pages.*

Directions: *Using the* Yellow Pages *of your local phone directory, list the names and phone numbers of at least two suppliers for each of the following products and services.*

1. Advertising Agencies and Counselors

_____

_____

_____

2. Limousine Services

_____

_____

_____

3. Tire Dealers

_____

_____

_____

4. Movers

_____

_____

_____

5. Restaurants

_____

_____

_____

■ USING PHONE DIRECTORIES

The first step in locating a phone number of a business or residence is to know its name and correct spelling. Residence listings are arranged alphabetically by the last name. First names appear below each last name, also in alphabetical order.

Business listings are arranged alphabetically. If a person's name represents the company name, the entry will be under the last name (for example, *DENHAM Anne atty*). Otherwise, the company name will be listed under its first major word (for example, *Music Extravaganza The*).

Rules for Alphabetizing and Organizing Business or Resident Names

Study the following rules on how directory entries are alphabetized and organized.

- **A name may be listed in alternate ways.** For example, suppose you find that Lawrence David's phone number is not listed under *David, Lawrence* as you expect. The name may be listed as *Lawrence, David* (assuming you have reversed the names) or *David L.* Common first names may be abbreviated; for example, *William, Robert,* and *Thomas* may be shown as *Wm, Robt,* and *Thos,* respectively.

- **An ampersand (&), hyphen (-), and apostrophe (') are overlooked in alphabetizing.** Names such as *Martin & Mason, Martin-Miller,* and *Martin's Consulting Firm* are listed in alphabetic order without considering the ampersand (&), hyphen (-), or apostrophe ('). The underlined part of the following listings was considered in alphabetizing.

    <u>Martin K</u>erry

    <u>Martin & M</u>ason

    <u>Martin-Mi</u>ller Jeffrey

    <u>Martin's C</u>onsulting Firm

    <u>Martin's Di</u>ner

- **An initial precedes first names that begin with that initial.** The initial *N* representing a first name would appear before the first names *Nathan* and *Nicole.* Study this example:

    STEVENS A

      Anna

      E

      Emerson

      Emily

- **A name in all-capital letters appears at the beginning of its letter section.** These entries would be found at the beginning of the *W* section.

    WABG Radio

    WCNE TV

    WSI Wallpapers

- **A number in a name is alphabetized as if it were spelled out as a word.** A number will be shown as a number in its listing (if that is the official format in the company or organization name). However, the number will be alphabetized as though it were spelled out as a word. For example:

    Saw Mill Cafe

    7 Seas Restaurant

    Silver Spoon Inn

    Soup to Nuts Lunch Stop

- **A prefix in a name is considered part of the name.** Names with prefixes are not listed separately. The underlined part in these listings shows how the entries were alphabetized.

Macadamia Nut House

MacDonald's Kitchen

Mackenzie's Market

McDonald's of Cornish

- **A common abbreviation is alphabetized as if it were spelled out.** For example, *St. George's Church* would be alphabetized as if it were spelled *Saint George's Church.* The underlined part in these listings shows how the entries were alphabetized.

ST Clair David

SAINT Geneva

ST JEAN Carl & Barbara

- **The word *the* at the beginning of an organization name is not considered in alphabetizing.** The company *The Musical Store,* for example, would be listed under the letter *M.* Study these examples:

Muse Barbara LISW

Music Box Retreat The

Music Junction

Musical Store The

- **A cross-reference may list common spelling variations.** At the beginning of the list of names, a cross-reference may direct you to other spellings. For example, the name *Smith* has variations like *Smythe* and *Smithe.* For example, you may see:

SMITH—See also Schmidt, Schmind, Schmitt, Smyth, Smythe

Using Personal Directories

A personal directory is your own record of frequently called numbers. Common formats are an electronic list or database on a computer, a small book with alphabetical listings, a rotary file on your desk, or electronic lists stored on your cell phone. Whatever format you use, be sure your personal directory is current, easy to read, and easily accessible.

Using Company Directories

Many companies publish directories to make internal communication easier and more efficient. Formats include electronic lists, or databases, and hard copies in looseleaf binders. These directories may list phone numbers by department, alphabetic lists of employees, and employees' extensions. An *extension* is usually a two-, three-, or four-digit number.

Using Directories to Make International Calls

Today it is simple to dial anywhere in the world. In fact, most international calls can be dialed direct. Most long-distance companies handle international calls. If yours does not, locate a service provider who does. Your phone directory may list a special number to call for information on these companies.

To make an international call, you will need to dial an international access code, a country code, a city code, and finally the local number. Most phone directories include a list of the country codes and city codes for major foreign cities. These directories also explain how to make an international call. Dial each number carefully and slowly. Notify the international call provider if you reach an incorrect number; you should receive credit on charges for the call.

■ USING DIRECTORY ASSISTANCE

Directory assistance is convenient and helpful, but using it may add charges to your phone bill. First try one of these options for locating phone numbers: use your phone directory, refer to a list of frequently called numbers, or access the local *White Pages* or *Yellow Pages* database provided by your local phone company.

When the above options are impossible, unsuccessful, or impractical, use ***directory assistance.*** Directory assistance provides access to many numbers. When you dial the directory assistance number, a recording will assist you with locating a number and/or an address. Usually you must give the name of the city where the business or residence you are seeking is located. Then the operator or a recording will provide the information.

You may also dial 411 for assistance about a specific number, and you may dial 911 for emergency assistance.

Most phone companies limit the number of times you can use directory assistance in a certain period without incurring charges. A charge is incurred for each use beyond the limit. In addition, phone companies often limit the number of items you can request per call. For example, you may be allowed to make two requests per call (such as telephone number and address) and three calls within a given period of time (usually the customer's billing period). Check with your local phone service provider about these policies, which are usually located in the front of a phone directory.

Keep in mind that an extra charge is usually incurred whenever an operator is involved in your call.

ACTIVITY 2-3

Locating Phone Numbers

Purpose: To help you determine the correct reference for locating phone numbers.

Directions: *Indicate where you would most likely find the phone numbers for the following people or businesses. Use choices "a" through "e" for your responses.*

      a. Personal phone directory

      b. Company phone directory

      c. Local Yellow Pages

      d. Local White Pages

      e. Directory assistance

_____ **1.** Your carpool members

_____ **2.** A company that sells computer supplies

_____ **3.** The name of your local doctor

_____ **4.** A list of coworkers

_____ **5.** Cornish Station Restaurant in Cornish

_____ **6.** The name of your closest florist

_____ **7.** The Human Resources Department

_____ **8.** The name of a friend whose number you lost and whose name you cannot locate in the local or your personal telephone directory

_____ **9.** A car dealer

_____ **10.** Polina Olanovich, a possible customer, living in Old Orchard Beach

Other Types of Operator-Assisted Calls

Collect calls:
0 + Area Code + number

Collect Calls   In a ***collect call*** the person called agrees to pay the charges. To activate this type of call, dial 0 + Area Code + phone number. If you hear programmed instructions, listen to and follow them carefully. If an operator answers, say you are making a collect call, then give your name and the recipient's name. The operator will dial the person's number, say who is calling, and verify whether the recipient will accept the charges for the call. If the recipient agrees, the operator will leave the line. If the recipient does not agree, the operator cannot complete the call.

Third-number billing:
0 + Area Code + number

Third-Number Billing   ***Third-number billing*** bills a long-distance call to a phone besides the one you are calling to or from. To activate this type of call, dial 0 + Area Code + phone number. You might reach an automated system. If you reach an automated system, listen to and follow the directions. If an operator comes on the line, say you wish to charge the call to a third number and give that number with area code. In some situations, the operator may verify whether the third-number party will accept the charges. If no confirmation is received, the operator cannot complete the call unless you make other billing arrangements.

Person-to-person calls:
0 + Area Code + number

Person-to-Person Calls   A ***person-to-person call*** allows you to speak only with a specific person (in some cases, an extension). You will need operator assistance to make a person-to-person call. To make a person-to-person call, dial 0 + Area Code + phone number.

Making Calls with Cell Phones

Cell phones are widely used today as a wireless option for making calls from almost any location covered by the service provider. Depending on your needs, you can select a variety of features that allow you to communicate both words and pictures to your voice and/or e-mail via your computer wherever you are at the time.

Keep these important points in mind when you are making calls using cell phones:

1. Find a location that will accept your cell phone BEFORE you make the call recognizing that open areas usually work better than others.

2. If you are driving and need to make a call with your cell phone, pull over to the side of the road or into a parking lot. Failure to do so can result in very serious accidents. Cell phones can be mounted in your vehicle to create a speakerphone situation for communication while driving.

3. Turn off your cell phone when you are in meetings or social events where it would be an interruption.

4. Familiarize yourself with your cell phone and its special features.

5. Avoid using cell phones when the nature of the call you are making is CONFIDENTIAL.

Making Calls from Planes

Making calls from planes using phones installed in the plane is convenient. Some planes have phones attached to each seat. Others have phones that are available in designated areas of the plane. Keep these important points in mind when you are making calls from phones installed in planes:

1. Recognize that privacy will be limited. Keep your voice low so that you do not disturb others near you.

2. Read the instructions for using phones installed in planes BEFORE you try to make a call. Otherwise, you run the risk of unexpected time wasted and the possibility of additional cost.

3. Write down the points you intend to cover in the call BEFORE you make the call to save yourself time and money.

4. Be alert for any special instructions from the crew that might be an interference when you are considering making a call in a plane.

next slide

Conference Calls   *Conference calls* permit three or more parties to communicate on a single call, which saves time and costs. Conference calls may be any combination of local or long-distance calls. They usually require operator assistance. When you arrange a conference call, provide the operator with the names and numbers of all the parties involved and a time that the call is to occur. Allow a few minutes for all the parties to be connected.

Your phone system may enable you to complete a conference call yourself. Check first with your service provider before requesting operator assistance.

■ PHONE SERVICES

Many phone services are available and vary by geographic location. Some people prefer to have basic phone services; others prefer advanced features. Some are available at no charge, and some services have a fee.

Calling Card   A *calling card* is a card assigned to an individual or a phone number. With a calling card, you can make calls from almost any location in the United States without coins and with little or no operator assistance. Calling cards are provided by most major long-distance phone companies. Charges for calls made with a calling card appear on the monthly phone bill.

Prepaid Phone Card   A *prepaid phone card* can make the process of calling more convenient. Similar to a calling card, it allows the user to make phone calls without coins, because the charges are paid for in advance. Usually an access code or number must be dialed to begin processing the call. Prepaid phone cards are available from many sources and in various allotments of time or dollar amounts.

Directory Listing   *Phone-number-only* service allows you to list your name and home number and just a portion or none of your address in the directory. Some customers prefer not to list their addresses for security reasons.

Two-Person Directory Listing   This allows two people with the same last name living at the same address to list both of their first names in the directory at no charge. For example:

MATHEWS Sebastian & Veronica

Often this service offers a "distinctive ring" pattern to identify who the call is for.

ACTIVITY 2-4

Choosing Operator-Assisted Phone Services

Purpose: To help you analyze and choose appropriate operator-assisted phone services.

Directions: *Assume that you want to make each of the calls below. For each call, indicate the most appropriate service from the list provided. Write the letter of your selection in the spaces provided (more than one selection may be appropriate).*

       a. *Direct-dial (station-to-station)*

       b. *Person-to-person*

       c. *Collect*

       d. *Calling card*

       e. *Third-number billing*

       f. *Toll-free 800 number*

       g. *International direct-dial*

       h. *International operator-assisted*

       i. *Cell*

       j. *Conference*

_i_   **1.** You are driving the company car to pick up an order at a printer. On your way back to the office, you are delayed because of a major accident on your route.

_a_   **2.** You want to call your Uncle Emerson, who lives only a few blocks from you.

_e_   **3.** You are at a coin-operated phone and need to call your office. You have no change.

_c_   **4.** You are at the airport without your calling card and need to reach a business associate at her home. You have no change, but you know that your administrative assistant is in the office today.

_b_   **5.** You are traveling on business and need to speak to Elizabeth Littlejohn—and only Elizabeth!—who is handling your travel itinerary.

_a_   **6.** You wish to call your partner on her cellular phone.

_c_   **7.** Your want to phone home from a business trip (long-distance), but you have no money. You know that your mother is visiting at your home.

_j_   **8.** You need to speak with several business associates at the same time.

_g_   **9.** You want to call your manager in London, and you have his telephone number handy.

_a_   **10.** You want to speak to your close friend, who lives 350 miles away.

Additional Optional Services

The following optional services carry a monthly charge that varies with the geographic location. Your local phone directory or phone company can provide further information on the charges within your area.

Nondirectory Listed Number   With *nondirectory listed number* service, your phone number will not appear in the phone directory but will be available from directory assistance.

Nonpublished Number   With *nonpublished number* service, your phone number will not appear in the phone directory and will not be released by directory assistance.

Additional Listing   With *additional listing* service, several people with the same phone number may each have a separate listing in the directory. Usually it is possible to request as many listings as desirable for an individual phone number.

Optional Calling Services

Call Waiting   *Call waiting* is a service that alerts you, while you are on a call, that you have an incoming call. With call waiting, you will hear a quiet beeping tone during the current call. You can then place the first call on hold in order to answer the second call; doing so ensures that you never miss a call. With a similar service, *selective call waiting,* you can temporarily cancel the call-waiting tone so that it will not interrupt the current conversation.

Call Forwarding   *Call forwarding* is a service that allows you to transfer incoming calls to another number. This service is helpful if you are going to be unavailable at your usual number. Some systems provide *busy call forwarding,* which transfers incoming calls automatically when the line called is busy. *Delayed call forwarding* transfers calls automatically if the phone is not answered within a specified number of rings.

Speed Dialing   *Speed Dialing* allows you to dial frequently called local and long-distance numbers automatically. You must use a code or series of codes that are programmed into the phone. Instead of dialing the full number, you can dial the one- or two-digit code that you establish for the full number. Similar to speed calling, some phones *redial* the last number called when a special key is pressed or a code is entered.

Busy Redial   A *busy redial* service redials the last number called when that line is no longer busy. This service checks the line for several minutes, eliminating the need to redial repeatedly. The connection will be completed when you pick up the receiver.

Call Pickup   A *call pickup* service enables an individual to pick up an incoming call on any telephone within a system (such as a company). The user must enter a code to pick up the call. Other users within the system can continue to use their phones as usual. The call pickup feature eliminates the need for the individual to answer a call in his or her own office. It also eliminates the need to have several lines on each telephone.

Individual Call Transfer   *Individual call transfer* enables a user to transfer a call to another phone without an operator's help. This saves time for users and operators.

Conference Calling   A *conference calling* service permits three or more persons to communicate on a single call. Some phone systems enable you to make conference calls without operator assistance.

Caller ID   *Caller ID* displays the number of an incoming call on a special panel or device. This panel or device is available through the phone provider. For a fee, you can also add Call Intercept if the number is unavailable and send it to Home Voice mail.

Call Trace   *Call trace* determines the source of, or traces, the most recent incoming call. This service is helpful for tracing obscene or harassing phone calls.

Call Blocking   *Call blocking* eliminates the display of your number on any Caller ID display device or panel.

■ TIME AND CHARGES

Time costs money, especially on the phone. Phone charges can include the cost of the phone itself, features, services, and time used. These costs vary by company and situation.

Local calls may be billed per call, based on the length of the call. Local calls also may be billed at a flat monthly fee. Many providers bill one month in advance for local service.

Long-distance calls are billed separately from local calls. Rates for long-distance calls are based on several factors. These include the call's destination, day of the week, time of day, length of the conversation, and any operator services requested. Direct-dial long-distance calls cost less than operator-assisted calls. Operator-assisted calls made during the normal business day usually are the most costly.

Several companies offer long-distance services. Their rates are competitive and vary considerably. Before you select a long-distance company, consider the services you need and the cost of them.

Economizing Long-Distance Calls

You can economize the cost of long-distance calls by doing the following:

Schedule lengthy long-distance calls in advance.   You will be more likely to reach the person you are calling. In addition, you might be able to call when rates are lower. Remember that rates are most expensive during normal business hours.

Schedule conference calls in advance.   All parties can be prepared when you plan ahead.

Use your phone directory (print or electronic version) before calling directory assistance.   Avoid directory assistance charges by locating phone numbers yourself.

Get credit on your bill for service-related errors and problems.   Ask the operator for credit on calls that have poor connections (interference), calls that go through to wrong numbers, and loss of service.

S U M M A R Y

1. Think about your phone skills when you make a phone call. An awareness of your skills will help you improve them.

2. Proper attitude is crucial to making a successful and positive phone call.

3. Before you make a call, be mentally and physically ready to initiate it and know the purpose of it.

4. Continue to plan the call as it progresses.

5. Have the necessary materials, such as account numbers, catalogs, and other applicable information, at your fingertips before you make the call.

6. Before you make a call, consider your own readiness and the time of day. Refer to the time zone map in your phone directory to verify the time difference between your location and the recipient's.

7. If you cannot find a phone number in a local, personal, or other phone directory, call directory assistance for help.

8. A local phone directory is sometimes called the *White Pages.* This directory provides an alphabetic listing of names and phone numbers and other phone reference information.

9. Use the *Yellow Pages* when you need to locate a product or service. If you cannot locate information on a particular topic in the *Yellow Pages,* search under related headings or subjects.

10. The first step in locating the phone number of a business or residence is to know its name and its correct spelling.

11. A personal directory is your own record of frequently called numbers.

12. Most phone directories include a list of the country codes and city codes for major foreign cities. These directories also explain how to make an international call. In addition to the codes, some directories list the time difference from a specific time zone to other countries.

13. Keep in mind that an extra charge is usually incurred whenever an operator is involved in your call.

14. Conference calls permit three or more parties to communicate on a single call, which saves time and costs.

15. Many phone services are available and vary by geographic location.

16. Use technology whenever possible to assist you in locating numbers.

17. Be aware of privacy concerns when using a cell phone.

18. Phone charges can include the cost of the phone itself, features, services, and time used. These costs vary by company and situation.

▌ APPLICATION ACTIVITY 2–1

Which Optional Calling Service Should Be Used?

Directions: *Identify the Optional Calling Service that would be most efficient to use in the description provided by writing in the correct answer.*

a. Call waiting

b. Call forwarding

c. Speed dialing

d. Busy redial

e. Call pickup

f. Individual call transfer

g. Conference calling

h. Caller ID/Call intercept

i. Call trace

j. Call blocking

1. You would use _____ if you wanted to display the number of an incoming call on a special panel or device. For a fee, you could add _____ _____if the number is unavailable and send it to your Home Voice Mail if that option is available.

2. You could use _____ _____ to allow you to dial numbers automatically programmed into the phone.

3. An optional calling service that keeps trying the last number called when that line is no longer busy is called _____ _____.

4. _____ _____ is a service that allows you to transfer incoming calls to another number.

5. A service that alerts you while you are on a call that you have an incoming call is called _____ _____.

6. A _____ _____ service permits three or more persons to communicate on a single call.

▌ APPLICATION ACTIVITY 2–2

Using Your Phone Directory

Directions: *Use your local phone directory to find the answers to the questions below. Write your answers in the spaces provided.*

1. Which geographic region and area code(s) are covered by your local directory?

South Shore 902

_____

_____

2. If you have a question concerning your phone bill, what number should you call?

1-866-4ALIANT

3. How would you call directory assistance for the state of West Virginia?

1-902-555-1212

4. How would you call directory assistance for your local area?

411

5. If it is 4 p.m. in New York, what time is it in Arizona?

6. What is the area code for each city listed below?

a. Freeport, Maine

b. Cincinnati, Ohio

c. Las Vegas, Nevada

d. San Juan, Puerto Rico

7. What is the name of the time zone in which the state of Missouri is located?

8. What is the country code for each country listed below?

a. Spain

b. New Zealand

c. Denmark

d. Mexico

9. What is the city code for each city listed below?

a. Barcelona, Spain

b. Wellington, New Zealand

c. Copenhagen, Denmark

d. Mexico City, Mexico

10. List three community service groups that are listed in your phone directory.

APPLICATION ACTIVITY 2-3

Paying Less for More

Directions: *Based on the information you have studied in Chapter 2, suggest ways to save money on each of the following calls.*

1. Bob Rosberg calls directory assistance at least 12 times a month for numbers that are listed in the phone directory.

    _____

    _____

    _____

    _____

2. Ty Mongoluksana arranged a conference call at the last minute. Two of the five parties were unavailable and the call had to be postponed.

    _____

    _____

    _____

    _____

3. Esther Stevens always rushes when she makes a call. Consequently, she frequently reaches an incorrect number and has to call again.

    _____

    _____

    _____

    _____

4. Helen Rankin has known for nearly a week that she would have to speak with a supplier for at least an hour. The supplier is located a thousand miles away, and she makes a person-to-person call to make sure she reaches him.

    _____

    _____

    _____

    _____

5. Anna Stoit frequently calls her mother long-distance during her lunch hour to chat. She charges the calls to her home telephone number.

    _____

    _____

    _____

    _____

CASE STUDY 2.1

The Confused Caller

Directions: *Analyze the situation described below. Then answer the questions that follow.*

It's a late Monday afternoon, and you are waiting in the reception area of your dentist's office for your appointment. The dentist, Dr. Hatch, is running nearly 30 minutes behind on his appointments.

As you wait, you observe the receptionist, Jill. Her desk is a mess, piled high with folders, copies of bills, checks, pens, envelopes, and Dr. Hatch's appointment book. Jill's computer is positioned too high for her to sit comfortably at it. Each time the telephone rings—and it usually rings four times before Jill answers it—she has to rummage around her desktop to find message forms and a pen that works. Often she needs Dr. Hatch's appointment book and cannot find it; when she does locate it, she has to go through several pages to locate the current month. In addition, as patients are arriving and leaving, it takes Jill additional time to deal with them because of her disorganization.

Finally, Dr. Hatch appears and says, "Jill, please call my appointments from 2 p.m. on and reschedule them. I will take care of the patients who are here, but I'm not feeling well. 1 just can't stay until 5 o'clock."

Jill replies, "Yes, Dr. Hatch. I may not be able to reach all of them at this late hour, but I'll try."

Jill begins to call the six patients who are scheduled from 2 p.m. on. For the next half hour, she is on the phone, trying to notify patients and reschedule their appointments. You notice that she has to locate the phone numbers within the patients' folders. Several of the folders are located in the mess on her desk. As she continues, she has difficulty reaching several patients because several of the home numbers do not have answering machines and she does not have their work numbers handy. In her growing anxiety, Jill mistakenly calls two patients who do not have appointments that day. At the end of the half hour, she has reached only three of the six patients.

As Jill pauses between calls, you ask her how much longer she thinks you will have to wait. You are already late getting back to work. Jill offers to call your office and tell them you are delayed. Near the end of Jill's conversation with your office, Dr. Hatch comes into the waiting room to ask why the next patient has not been sent in. In her confusion, Jill hangs up her phone before ending the call. You leave, deciding to call at a later time to reschedule.

1. Why is the arrangement of Jill's desk interfering with her ability to process calls?

   _____

   _____

   _____

   _____

   _____

   _____

2. What suggestions could you offer Jill for improving the way she keeps track of phone numbers?

_____

_____

_____

_____

_____

_____

3. What additional information about patients should Jill record in order to be sure she can reach them during the working hours?

_____

_____

_____

_____

_____

_____

4. How does Jill's preoccupation with making the calls to patients affect her other job responsibilities?

_____

_____

_____

_____

_____

5. How do you think Jill should have handled your problem concerning the lateness of your appointment?

_____

_____

_____

_____

6. What should Jill do to avoid reaching wrong numbers?

_____

_____

_____

_____

_____

7. What is your overall response to this case study?

_____

_____

_____

_____

_____

CASE STUDY 2.2

"Are You There?"

Directions: _Read Case Study 2 described below. Answer the questions that follow._

Sam is so excited—he has just purchased his first cell phone. He had carefully reviewed all the orientation assistance provided by the service provider, A-OK Cell Phone. He is now happily on his way in his new car, a bright red Corvette convertible. Life is good!

As Sam is driving out of the parking lot at the local mall, he decides that he needs to call his mother and see if he can operate his cell phone properly. He punches in his mother's number and gets a busy signal. Oh well, Sam thought, she is on the phone with someone. He then decides to call his sister who is working at a nearby restaurant. She also owns a cell phone. He punches in that number, but gets a recorded message that he has dialed an "unavailable number."

At this very moment, Sam swerves his Corvette only to hear loud brakes and a crash. His front fender has been bumped by another vehicle—an elderly man driving an old pickup truck that looks at least 15 years old! He jumps out and starts a conversation with the driver concerning who is at fault, only to realize that this is not working.

Then Sam needs to call the police. Out comes the cell phone. He presses 911 and gets help. Thank goodness for the cell phone.

1. Why did having a cell phone to call 911 help Sam?

_____

_____

_____

2. Do you feel that Sam really understood how to operate his cell phone? Explain briefly.

_____

_____

_____

3. What steps should Sam take before he uses his cell phone again?

_____

_____

_____

4. Have you experienced any problems using a cell phone? If so, explain briefly how you have handled the problems.

_____

_____

_____

5. What did you learn from reading this case study? Be as specific as possible.

_____

_____

_____

Handling Incoming Phone Calls

"The most valuable of all talents is that of never using two words when one will do."
—**Thomas Jefferson**

CHAPTER OBJECTIVES

Chapter 3 will help you:

1. Answer the phone professionally.

2. Screen calls professionally and efficiently.

3. Place callers on hold professionally.

4. Transfer calls efficiently.

5. Record messages accurately.

6. Leave messages efficiently on answering machines or other recording equipment.

PICTURE THIS

Your phone rings while you are on another call. Your caller identification indicates that this is an important call being returned. Meanwhile, the call you are currently on is equally important. What should you do?

_____

_____

_____

■ PREPARING FOR INCOMING CALLS

Be prepared! Keep the following important points in mind:

1. Arrange your work area to include the necessary materials. Have pens and message forms readily available.

2. Place a clock within sight for immediate reference.

3. Place your phone in a convenient location. If you are right-handed, place the phone on the left side of your work area, so you can use your right hand to take messages. Do the reverse if you are left-handed.

4. Use a phone headset if you are using the phone constantly and/or if you need access to a computer for keying messages electronically.

5. Keep phone directories and lists of frequently used phone numbers, extensions, e-mail addresses, and fax numbers readily available. If you have this information stored electronically, have a printed copy available in case of power outages or computer failure.

6. When you need to be away from your work area, make arrangements to have any calls answered. Using an ***answering machine*** can provide this service for you. Answering machines can be configured with messages that can be updated daily to reflect your work schedule to the caller as well as procedures for leaving a message. With some phone systems, you can automatically route incoming calls directly to another person until you return to your work area. Above all, be sure that you return or take appropriate action on any messages left on your answering machine. Failure to do so can result in loss of business or goodwill with callers, whatever the reason for their calling.

7. If you are using a cell phone, be sure the phone is in working order to handle incoming calls.

Be prepared for incoming calls. Have your phone, message forms, pens, phone directories, and other references readily available.

Even when you are away from your desk, have a method in place for answering your incoming calls.

■ ANSWERING THE PHONE

When you answer the phone, create a sense of being comfortable in speaking with the caller, and be pleasant. This will help you during the call and when concluding it.

The Robot Receptionist

"Thank you for calling the XYZ Company. If you are calling from a touch-tone phone, please press 1 to place an order, press 2 to. . . ." You hear such messages frequently—the voice of a machine known as an *automated attendant*. In other words, it is a robot receptionist. A robot receptionist is desirable when:

- Human receptionists are scarce and/or expensive.
- The receptionist is unavailable.
- Human operators need time to handle the calls that generate sales rather than merely transmitting routine information.

  An effective automated attendant system increases the capacity to handle incoming calls.

Keep these points in mind to help you answer incoming calls.

- **Answer your phone immediately, preferably no later than the second ring.** This shows that you are efficient and attentive thus avoiding frustration on the part of the callers.

- **Identify yourself in a friendly and professional manner.** This will begin the conversation pleasantly and positively.

  "Good morning, Dr. Santos' office. How may I help you?"

- **Use the caller's name if you know it.** When you use the caller's name during the call, it affirms a sense of warmth and personal interest.

  "Thank you for calling, Joyce. I will be sure that Dr. Hatch receives your message."

- **Obtain as much information as you can from the caller to help you process the call.** Practice good questioning techniques and speak clearly. Obtain as much information as possible from the caller to reduce the need to transfer calls. For example, say,

  "I will be glad to give Mrs. Chin your message. May I have your name, address, and phone number, please."

- **Do not interrupt the caller. Write one or two words on your message form that will remind you to focus on a point.** Ask your questions or make your comments when the caller stops talking.

- **Give accurate information.** If any information is unclear or you have insufficient answers to the caller's questions, say that you need the necessary information. Avoid using vague phrases, such as

  "I really am not sure" or

  "It may be that."

You never get a second chance to make a good first impression.

Identifying Yourself

First impressions count. When identifying yourself on the phone, your tone of voice sends an immediate and lasting message. A pleasant and cheerful "Good afternoon, Dearborn Enterprises," as opposed to a curt "Dearborn Enterprises, hold," sets the scene for a positive phone call.

The wording of a professional and courteous identification depends on your organization and skill. You may be answering the phone for one of many departments, for another person, or for yourself.

Follow these steps to ensure that you properly identify yourself on the phone.

- **Identify yourself courteously.**

  "Customer Service, Miss Rivers. May I help you?"

  "Dr. Nash's office; this is Jill. How may I help you?"

- **Use positive phrases when identifying yourself.**

  "Good morning, Branson Enterprises."
  "Cornish Bank and Trust Company; this is June."

- **Generate enthusiasm as you answer and identify yourself.**

  This will create a pleasant atmosphere for the entire call.

- **Smile when you answer a phone call.**

  Smiling throughout the call loosens your vocal chords, making you feel more relaxed.

ACTIVITY 3–1

Identify Yourself When Answering the Phone

Purpose: To practice identifying yourself properly when you answer the phone.

Directions: *Read each description and write an appropriate identification to use for incoming calls on the answer rules. Remember that an accurate identification when answering a phone can reduce the need to repeat information—thereby helping to ensure a positive conversation.*

1. Lisa Hale is an administrative assistant answering the phone for her manager, Elaine Hopkins.

   _____

   _____

   _____

   _____

2. Alan Wadsworth is a receptionist at the main switchboard of Barrens, Noble, and Quinn law firm.

   _____

   _____

   _____

   _____

3. Jack Vachenko is a clerk in Shipping and Receiving at the Portland, Maine, branch of Jordanski's Department Store.

   _____

   _____

   _____

   _____

4. Laurel Anderson from the Marketing Department of The L. R. Green Company is answering the phone of her co-worker, Jean Sturgeon.

   _____

   _____

   _____

   _____

5. Miriam Stolt is a sales associate in the Art Department of the Warwick Craft Store.

   _____

   _____

   _____

   _____

Next slide

Screening Calls

Learning to *screen* phone calls efficiently involves applying sound judgment and practice. After you have identified yourself, give the caller an opportunity to respond with his identification and purpose for calling.

When you are answering phone calls on behalf of a business or, more specifically, for another person, you need to immediately determine HOW to screen the call by checking in advance with the exact procedure used for screening calls.

Screening an Unwanted Caller   When you are answering the phone on behalf of someone else who does not wish to be interrupted, it is critical that your screening skills be exemplary. In the following situation, Kendra Nye is working on a project that must be completed by the end of the day. Kendra has told her administrative assistant, Roberta Douglas, she does not want to be interrupted unless Marie Orsini calls. Roberta screens the caller as follows.

Discuss

Roberta: "Ms. Nye's office, this is Roberta speaking."

Caller: "This is Ken Murphy from Murphy Consulting. May I speak with Kendra Nye, please?"

Roberta: "I'm sorry, Mr. Murphy, Ms. Nye is not available at the moment. May I have her call you?"

Caller: "Yes, please. My number is 555-3221."

Roberta: "Thank you, Mr. Murphy. I'll give Ms. Nye your number. That's **555**-3221."

Caller: "Yes, thank you. Good-bye."

Roberta: "Good-bye."

Let's Analyze It   Roberta was professional and diplomatic with the caller. She said nothing to reveal that Ms. Nye was in the office but did not want to speak with him. Shortly after this call, Marie Orsini called, and Roberta transferred the call to Ms. Nye immediately.

Screening an Unidentified Caller   When a caller refuses to give their identity, it is extremely important to screen the call carefully, as in this example:

Discuss

Roberta: "Ms. Nye's office, Roberta speaking."

Caller: "May I speak with Kendra Nye?"

Roberta: "May I ask who is calling?"

Caller: "Just connect me to Kendra. She knows me."

Roberta: "I'm sorry, but Ms. Nye is not available at the moment. Would you like to leave a message?"

Caller: "Uh, no. I'll call back later. Bye."

Roberta: "Good-bye."

Let's Analyze It   Roberta was courteous throughout the call. She gave the caller an opportunity to leave a message. What happens if the caller phones again later in the day when Ms. Nye is available? Roberta knows that Ms. Nye will not take any calls unless she knows who is calling.

Roberta: "Ms. Nye's office, Roberta speaking."

Caller: "Hello, may I speak with Kendra Nye?"

Roberta: "May I ask who is calling?"

Caller: "That's OK; just put me through to Kendra. I'm a personal friend of hers."

Roberta: "I'm sorry, but I cannot put a call through to Ms. Nye without knowing who is calling."

Caller: "Oh, all right. This is Robert Rubin from Tri-County Sports."

Roberta: "Thank you, Mr. Rubin. I'll see if Ms. Nye is available."

Let's Analyze It   Roberta was courteous but firm in insisting that the caller identify himself. She can now inform Ms. Nye that Mr. Rubin is on the line. If Ms. Nye does not wish to take the call, Roberta has left herself the option of telling Mr. Rubin that Ms. Nye is not available to speak with him at this time. Roberta could also offer Mr. Rubin the option of leaving a message on Ms. Nye's voice mail.

Handling Interruptions   Sometimes a caller will not accept the fact that the person they wish to speak with is unavailable. When this happens, you must remain professional yet be firm in screening the call. If the call is an emergency, you must locate the person immediately explaining the urgency of the call.

If you are not clear about the purpose of the call but the caller is insistent, ask the caller to hold while you determine whether the person being called is available. If the person is not available, ask if someone else might be able to help.

Know the wishes of those you screen calls for that are of a personal nature such as from family, personal friends, and designated business associates.

Using Discretion Wisely   Being *discreet* means that you are careful not to reveal any inappropriate information.

In the hypothetical situation of Ms. Nye and her administrative assistant, Roberta, one morning Ms. Nye was late for work because of traffic. She tried to call Roberta on her cell phone but was unable to get through because she was out of range for making calls. A call came in for Ms. Nye from her regional manager, Ron Brucia.

Roberta: "Good morning, Ms. Nye's office. This is Roberta, how may I help you?"

Mr. Brucia: "Hello, Roberta. This is Ron Brucia. Is Kendra there?"

Roberta: "I'm sorry, Mr. Brucia, but Kendra is not available at the moment. May I have her call you?"

Mr. Brucia: "Sure."

Roberta: "I'll have her call you as soon as possible."

Mr. Brucia: "Thanks, Roberta. Have a nice day."

Roberta: "Thank you, good-bye."

Let's Analyze It   Roberta was careful not to reveal any inappropriate information to Mr. Brucia. She did not say that Kendra was late. She simply said Kendra was unavailable.

The phrase "not available" safely covers a wide variety of situations in which the person called cannot come to the phone. An expert phone screener should apply this phrase tactfully when the situation presents itself.

ACTIVITY 3-2

Screening Calls

Purpose: To help you decide what to do when you screen a phone call.

Directions: *Read each situation and determine whether the call should be forwarded to the desired party. If it should be forwarded, place a check mark in the* Yes *column. If it should not be forwarded, place a check mark in the* No *column. Explain.*

	Yes	No
1. A woman, who refuses to identify herself or state her business, calls and wants to speak to Mr. Polito immediately.	_____	_____
2. Ms. Burnett, who had to do some personal errands, is late getting back from lunch. An important client calls and asks to speak with her.	_____	_____
3. Mr. Mazzaro is attending an important meeting in Ms. Googins office. His wife calls and tells you that she must speak to him because of a family emergency.	_____	_____
4. Mrs. Goldstein asks you to hold all of her calls for an hour. A client calls and asks to speak to her.	_____	_____
5. Mr. Quinn is on the phone with a client when his manager, Mr. Rowe, calls on another line and asks to speak with him.	_____	_____

Sample Responses for Incoming Calls

When the person called is in:

"Yes, just a moment and I will connect you."

When the person called is on another line:

"She's talking on another line. Would you care to hold, or may I have her call you?"

When the person called is not in:

"Mr. Tobey will not be in today. Can someone else help you, or would you like to leave a message on his voice mail?"

"Mr. Tobey will be out of town until next week. May I give him a message?"

"Dr. Nash is taking calls for Dr. Markson. I have that number if you would like it."

"The department is closed for the day. Business hours are from 8 to 4:30. Would you care to call tomorrow?"

"Ms. Scott is not available right now. Could someone else help you?"

"I'm sorry, she is not in the office right now. Would you care to leave a message?"

"He is away from his desk. May I ask him to call you?"

When screening a call:

"Will Mr. Lopez know what your call is about?"

"May I tell her what the call is about?"

"May I say who is calling, please?"

"Just a moment and I will try to locate him for you. (pause) I'm sorry, he is not available. Could someone else help you?"

When transferring a call:

"That department is located in another building. Just a moment and I will transfer your call. The number is 555-8899 if you wish to call them in the future."

"Mr. Hardwick is in charge of that department, and I am sure he can help you. Just a moment and I will transfer your call. In case we are disconnected, his extension is 445."

"Our Marketing Department can answer your question, just a moment and I will have your call transferred."

next slide

Put a caller on hold only after you have allowed him or her to speak.

Placing Callers on Hold

Sometimes it is necessary to place callers on *hold* so you can get information, speak to another person, or answer another call. Most phones have a specific procedure for placing callers on hold. Become familiar with the procedure for your phone so you do not accidentally cut off callers.

The act of putting someone on hold is not a mechanical operation. You must be both courteous and professional in the process. Never put a caller on hold before allowing him or her to speak. Wait until it is your turn to speak and then politely ask the caller to hold. See the following examples:

"One moment, please. Let me see if Ms. Edgerly is available."

"Please hold. Someone will be right with you."

"Would you mind holding for a moment, please. Another line is ringing."

Being placed on hold is not a particularly pleasant experience. This is true even when the phone system plays soft music or messages. When you return to the caller, express appreciation for waiting. You might say something like:

"Thank you for holding, Mr. Martinez. I have your report in front of me now."

"Thank you for holding, Mary. Mr. Wadsworth's line is still busy. Would you like to continue to hold, or would you prefer to leave a message?"

Both examples show that you are concerned about and interested in the caller's needs. The caller should not feel neglected or forgotten. Most people wait patiently on hold for approximately 15 to 30 seconds.

When receiving multiple calls at the same time, keep a list of each so that you can handle all of them efficiently.

Ideally, phone calls would be received one at a time. In reality, many calls are received at the same time. Answer the lines one at a time in the order in which they are received. You might need to place one or more of the calls on hold so that you can complete or transfer others. Before placing calls on hold, make a list of each call so that you can handle all of them efficiently. Beside each extension number, list the caller's name and a brief summary of the purpose of the call. (Transferring calls is explained later in this chapter.)

Professional Guidelines for Placing a Caller on Hold or Transferring a Call

- Let the caller know what you are doing and why.

- If a caller was on hold, be sure to express appreciation when you return to the call. "Thank you for waiting" tells the caller you are ready to resume the conversation.

- If the caller has been on hold for more than 30 seconds, check periodically to see if he or she wishes to keep waiting.

- If the call is long-distance, ask the caller for permission to put the call on hold or transfer it. Give the caller a choice.

- When transferring a call, explain briefly to the person why and to whom you are transferring the call. Let the caller know when you begin the transfer.

ACTIVITY 3-3

Placing Calls on and Removing Them from Hold

Purpose: To give you insight into the proper procedure for placing callers on hold and removing them from hold.

Directions: *Read the following examples of unprofessional phone conversations that may occur in an office. Then, write a more positive response for each example that would make the caller feel he or she is being treated courteously and professionally.*

1. **Recipient:** "Brandt Ludwig. Hold on, please."

   _____

   _____

   _____

   _____

2. **Recipient returning to caller placed on hold:** "Hello? Are you still there?"

   _____

   _____

   _____

   _____

3. **Caller:** "This is Santana Eastman. May I speak—"
   Recipient: "Would you hold, please?"

   _____

   _____

   _____

   _____

4. Recipient: "Burkowski's. Hold on, I have another call."

_____

_____

_____

_____

5. Recipient: "Kezar Falls Pizza Shop. We're busy; can you call back in 10 minutes? I'm on another line."

_____

_____

_____

_____

Transferring Calls

In certain situations, you may receive calls that should be directed to another person or department. When this happens, it is usually necessary to *transfer* the call. While transferring calls is very common, there are several important steps to keep in mind when transferring a call.

1. Become familiar with the function of each department within the business to which you might be transferring a call as well as the system and equipment you are using to transfer calls.

2. Keep a current company directory readily available, either electronically or printed, so that you can transfer the call accurately and quickly.

3. When you are unsure where the call should be transferred, place the caller on hold and get back to them shortly or offer to call them back with the correct information.

4. Before you transfer a call, tell the caller the person and/or department to whom you are transferring the call and the correct number and/or extension.

   "Mrs. Dearborn, I am transferring you to Customer Service. That number is 555-4001 in case you need this for future reference or if we should get disconnected."

5. Most phone systems allow you to speak privately to the person receiving the transferred call. In this case, summarize the caller's business so that the caller does not have to repeat the situation.

   "Elizabeth, I am transferring a call from Mrs. Dearborn. She is having a problem with her Create It software."

ACTIVITY 3-4

Analyzing Incoming Calls

Purpose: To practice analyzing and improving parts of phone conversations.

Directions: *Read each statement below and determine if it is acceptable. If it is, place a check mark in the* Yes *column. If it is not, place a check mark in the* No *column; then write a brief response as to why it is unacceptable. Explain.*

	Yes	No
1. "Maureen's not here right now. What's the message?" _____ _____ _____	_____	_____
2. "Hello. No, this is not Cornwall Hardware." _____ _____ _____	_____	_____
3. "Hold on, please; I'll transfer you. If we get disconnected, his extension is 5516." _____ _____ _____	_____	_____
4. "We don't deal with that item. Call the frame department." _____ _____ _____	_____	_____
5. "Good afternoon, this is Courtney's Bridal Shop. May I help you?" _____ _____ _____	_____	_____
6. "Mrs. Ginorio is at lunch and is 15 minutes overdue." _____ _____ _____	_____	_____

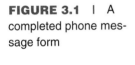

Taking Accurate Phone Messages

Today's technology provides a variety of options for taking phone messages. You may sit in front of a computer and key a message that is automatically forwarded to an electronic mailbox. You may leave an electronic message on voice mail, or you may be taking phone messages directly on paper. Whatever method used for taking a phone message, using efficient and positive communication skill is essential.

When the person called is unavailable, ask the caller if they would like to leave a message with you or on the person's voice mail. Follow these tips to help you take an accurate message:

1. If you are taking the message, *listen actively* and *ask questions* that will give you the necessary information in an efficient and professional manner.

2. As you are listening, try to detect the *tone* of the caller's voice.

3. Read numbers back to the caller in pairs to make sure you have recorded them correctly.

4. If necessary, verify any other questionable data and the spelling of names.

FIGURE 3.1 | A completed phone message form

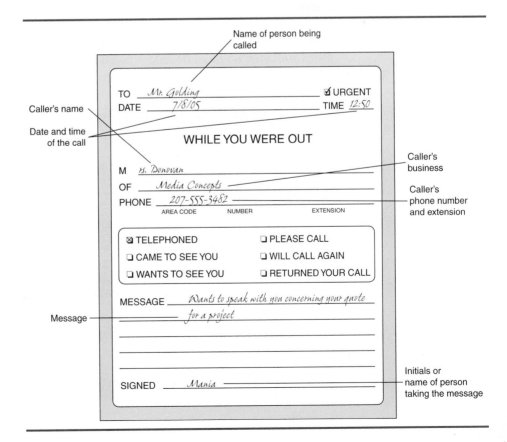

5. Repeat the entire message to the caller to be sure you have all the necessary details.

6. You may also inquire as to the urgency of the call. This can usually be determined by the caller's tone. Indicate whether the caller will call again or what other appropriate action needs to be taken.

Technology can provide you with the opportunity to have a caller's number automatically stored in memory for future reference. It is still a good idea to verify the number for accuracy.

If a caller does not wish to be identified, do not insist upon it. Write all the available information on the message and note "Will call again" on the message form.

Avoid **phone tag,** which results when two parties go back and forth trying to reach each other by phone. Tell the caller the best time to call again, or ask the caller for the best time to have the call returned. Phone tag can be expensive, wasting both time and money.

Once the message form is completed, deliver it promptly to the recipient. Most message forms are printed on colored paper for easy recognition. Be sure to place the message in a location where it will be readily noticed. If it is of a confidential nature, be sure to fold it and mark it properly. To be certain that all messages get delivered to the right person, establish and follow a predetermined procedure.

Phone tag can can be frustrating. To avoid it, note on messages the suggested times for returning calls.

ACTIVITY 3–5

Incomplete Messages

Purpose: To emphasize the importance of taking a complete phone message.

Directions: *For each item below, transfer the information to the message forms provided on page 65. After you have completed each message form, you will notice that important information is missing!*

1. Message for Laura Landry
   Lori Pike of Educational Visuals called.
   Please call her.
   February 23, 10:45 A.M.
   LL

2. Gregory Maxwell called.
   (601) 555-8734
   Please call him.
   April 17, 1:45 P.M.

3. Message for Chantel Pinewood
   Sam O'Conner from the Irish International Council called.
   (212) 555-3500
   Please call him about his passport.
   Jack

4. Message for Sue Parker
   Mike Pankowitz of the Portland Wordsmiths Book Store
   He will call back tomorrow.
   Sally

FIGURE 3.2

Call 1

TO _Laura Landry_

HERE IS A MESSAGE FOR YOU

Lori Pike

OF _Educational Visuals_

PHONE NO. _____ EXT. _____

- ❏ TELEPHONED
- ❏ RETURNED YOUR CALL
- ☑ PLEASE PHONE

- ❏ WILL CALL AGAIN
- ❏ CAME TO SEE YOU
- ❏ WANTS TO SEE YOU

| TAKEN BY _LL_ | DATE _Feb 23_ | TIME _10:45_ |

Call 2

TO _____

HERE IS A MESSAGE FOR YOU

Gregory Maxwell

OF _____

PHONE NO. _601-555-8734_ EXT. _____

- ❏ TELEPHONED
- ❏ RETURNED YOUR CALL
- ☑ PLEASE PHONE

- ❏ WILL CALL AGAIN
- ❏ CAME TO SEE YOU
- ❏ WANTS TO SEE YOU

| TAKEN BY | DATE _Feb. 17_ | TIME _1:45_ |

Call 3

TO _Chantel Pinewood_

HERE IS A MESSAGE FOR YOU

Sam 'O'Connel

OF _Irish International Council_

PHONE NO. _212-555-3500_ EXT. _____

- ❏ TELEPHONED
- ❏ RETURNED YOUR CALL
- ❏ PLEASE PHONE

- ❏ WILL CALL AGAIN
- ❏ CAME TO SEE YOU
- ❏ WANTS TO SEE YOU

Needs to know about his passport

| TAKEN BY _Jack_ | DATE | TIME |

Call 4

TO _Sue Parker_

HERE IS A MESSAGE FOR YOU

Mike Pankowitz

OF _Portland Wordsmiths' Book Store_

PHONE NO. _____ EXT. _____

- ❏ TELEPHONED
- ❏ RETURNED YOUR CALL
- ❏ PLEASE PHONE

- ☑ WILL CALL AGAIN
- ❏ CAME TO SEE YOU
- ❏ WANTS TO SEE YOU

Will call tomorrow

| TAKEN BY _Sally_ | DATE | TIME |

ACTIVITY 3-6

Taking Messages

Purpose: To practice recording complete messages based on information provided.

Directions: *For each call below, record a complete message, using the forms provided on page 67.*

1. On Friday, June 1, at 10:30 A.M. Pauline Snowman of the Bar Harbor Hotel called, asking to speak to Carlene Hatch. She wants to discuss the retirement party Ms. Miller is planning. Ms. Snowman can be reached at 555-3297 between 2 and 3 P.M. today.

2. You took a message for Katie Sargent at 12:19 on Wednesday, November 17, from a person identifying herself only as Suzanne. She said Katie would know who she was. She needs to speak to Katie as soon as possible. Katie should call her before 3:45 at 212-555-1208.

3. Peter Crosson received a call from Jessica Sefcik of the Map Center at 4:30 P.M. on Friday, June 1. Mr. Crosson had already left for the weekend when the call was received. Ms. Sefcik wants Peter to know she mailed the information he requested by express mail and he should receive it on Monday. If he has questions, he can call her on Monday at 301-555-2334.

4. Marilyn Williams of the Island Development Corporation called on July 3 at 10 A.M., asking to speak to Matthew Lukas. She wants him to call her on July 8 after 11 A.M. at 555-3400.

FIGURE 3.3

Call 1

TO _____ ❏ URGENT
DATE _____ TIME _____

WHILE YOU WERE OUT

M _____
OF _____
PHONE _____
　　　　　AREA CODE　　　NUMBER　　　EXTENSION

❏ TELEPHONED　　　　❏ PLEASE CALL
❏ CAME TO SEE YOU　　❏ WILL CALL AGAIN
❏ WANTS TO SEE YOU　❏ RETURNED YOUR CALL

MESSAGE _____
_____
_____
_____
_____

SIGNED _____

Call 2

TO _____ ❏ URGENT
DATE _____ TIME _____

WHILE YOU WERE OUT

M _____
OF _____
PHONE _____
　　　　　AREA CODE　　　NUMBER　　　EXTENSION

❏ TELEPHONED　　　　❏ PLEASE CALL
❏ CAME TO SEE YOU　　❏ WILL CALL AGAIN
❏ WANTS TO SEE YOU　❏ RETURNED YOUR CALL

MESSAGE _____
_____
_____
_____
_____

SIGNED _____

Call 3

TO _____ ❏ URGENT
DATE _____ TIME _____

WHILE YOU WERE OUT

M _____
OF _____
PHONE _____
　　　　　AREA CODE　　　NUMBER　　　EXTENSION

❏ TELEPHONED　　　　❏ PLEASE CALL
❏ CAME TO SEE YOU　　❏ WILL CALL AGAIN
❏ WANTS TO SEE YOU　❏ RETURNED YOUR CALL

MESSAGE _____
_____
_____
_____
_____

SIGNED _____

Call 4

TO _____ ❏ URGENT
DATE _____ TIME _____

WHILE YOU WERE OUT

M _____
OF _____
PHONE _____
　　　　　AREA CODE　　　NUMBER　　　EXTENSION

❏ TELEPHONED　　　　❏ PLEASE CALL
❏ CAME TO SEE YOU　　❏ WILL CALL AGAIN
❏ WANTS TO SEE YOU　❏ RETURNED YOUR CALL

MESSAGE _____
_____
_____
_____
_____

SIGNED _____

SUMMARY

1. The most important rule to prepare for incoming calls is, *Be prepared.*

2. Arrange your work area so that the materials necessary to receive incoming calls are available.

3. Voice mail is an automated system used to take incoming messages. If it is overused or if the recipient of the call does not follow up on messages, callers may become frustrated.

4. When you need to be away from your desk, make arrangements to have your incoming calls answered.

5. Some businesses use equipment that automatically answers phones that are not answered by an employee.

6. If the phone equipment you use records messages, remember to always play back and follow up your messages.

7. When you answer the phone, be pleasant thus creating a sense of being comfortable in speaking with the caller.

8. When identifying yourself on the phone, be aware that your tone of voice sends an immediate and lasting message.

9. The wording of a professional and courteous identification depends on your organization and your role within it.

10. Learning to screen calls positively takes practice. Screening calls also involves applying sound judgment.

11. Know when it is necessary to interrupt your manager.

12. Being discreet means that you are careful not to reveal any inappropriate information or too many details.

13. Most phones have a specific procedure for placing callers on hold. Become familiar with the procedure for your phone to avoid cutting off callers.

14. You must be courteous and professional in the process of putting someone on hold.

15. In order to transfer calls efficiently, learn the function of each department within your company.

16. Become thoroughly familiar with your phone system so you can transfer calls efficiently.

17. If you are taking a message, listen carefully and ask questions if you do not understand something. Record the information accurately.

18. Establish a procedure for leaving messages for those for whom you answer the phone.

APPLICATION ACTIVITY 3–1

Arranging a Workstation

Directions: *Analyze the situation described below and then answer the questions that follow.*

Grace Day is moving to a new office. Except for the phone, which is on the left side of the desk, and a computer terminal, which is on a computer table on the right, the workstation is empty. Grace is bringing the following items with her:

a. Pen and pencil holder

b. Pad of message forms

c. Company phone directory

d. Latest company product catalog and price lists

e. Rotary file that contains frequently used numbers

f. Extra pens and pencils

  g. Pad of 8 1/2″ × 11″ paper

  h. Ream of 8 1/2″ × 11″ white paper

  i. Envelopes

  j. Boxes of paper clips and staples

  k. Box of blank disks

  l. Copies of recent product advertisements

  m. Reference materials (dictionary, atlas, thesaurus)

1. Grace is right-handed. Should she move the phone? Why or why not?

_____

_____

_____

2. Write the letters of the items you think Grace will need to use when she takes notes or messages.

_____

3. Write the letters of the items you think Grace will need to use when she transfers a call.

_____

4. Write the letters of the items you think Grace will need to use when giving product information to a customer.

_____

5. Write the letters of the items you think Grace should place on top of the desk.

_____

Other comments: _____

_____

_____

_____

APPLICATION ACTIVITY 3-2

Screening Calls

Directions: *In the space provided, indicate how you would handle each of the following situations.*

1. You are answering the phone for Juliana, a co-worker, who left early for a doctor's appointment. Juliana receives a call from a supplier who has a question about a recent order.

_____

_____

2. Your manager is in his office interviewing a job applicant and has asked not to be disturbed. The president of the company calls and asks to speak to your manager, saying it is important. This has never happened before.

_____

_____

_____

3. You are managing the company switchboard, and an angry customer calls. He will not give his name or state his business. He insists on speaking to the president of the company, who is out of town.

_____

_____

_____

4. Your manager is working on some routine correspondence when her brother calls.

_____

_____

_____

5. Your manager has asked you to hold all of her calls except for Juanita McGregor, an important client. Ms. McGregor's business partner calls.

_____

_____

▎ APPLICATION ACTIVITY 3-3

Leaving Messages Efficiently on Answering Machines

Directions: _Read the situations below and write the messages you would leave on the answering machine._

Situation 1 You have been trying to reach your dentist to reschedule your appointment because of a conflict. Each time you call, the line is busy. Finally, you get through but only to the answering machine telling you that the office will be closed until the following Monday. The recording encourages you to leave a message and assures you that someone will get back to you as soon as possible. Create the message you would leave.

_____

_____

_____

_____

Situation 2   Your real estate agent called you earlier in the day to tell you that he has some "exciting" news to share with you concerning the possible sale of your property and asked you to get back to him as soon as possible. You are returning his call from your cell phone in the parking lot of a nearby restaurant. When you call, you get a recording with directions to leave a message. Create the message you would leave.

_____

_____

_____

_____

Situation 3   This morning you picked up the paper and noticed an ad for a used vehicle that caught your interest. The ad was adamant about the fact that "this one will not last long" so call immediately to reserve the opportunity for possible purchase. You call the toll-free number and get a recording which was very long and very involved. You listen intently and finally push the proper code only to now have to leave another message concerning your interest in the vehicle. Create the message you would leave.

_____

_____

_____

_____

_____

CASE STUDY 3.1

The Inconsiderate Representative

Directions: *Analyze the situation described below and then answer the questions that follow.*

Ariel Delaney has just been promoted to supervisor in the customer service department of a toy manufacturer. In her new position, she is responsible for overseeing the activities of three customer service representatives. On her second day on the job, Ariel overheard one of the representatives, Craig Albertson, making these comments and responses on the phone:

a. (*In the middle of a call*) "Excuse me, sir. Please hold."

b. (*Answering the other line*) "Playtime, please hold."

c. (*Returning to the first call*) "Hello? Are you still there? . . . What seems to be the problem, sir? . . . Did you check the package to make sure you received five connectors?"

d. "Only four connectors? Well, there should be five. Give me your name and address, and we'll send you another one."

e. "That's ZIP Code 2 0 0 3 4." (*Ending the call*)

f. (*Returning to the second call*) "Hello? Are you still there? May I help you?"

g. "Oh, you've got the wrong department. I'll transfer you."

After she heard this, Ariel was quite upset. She thought all representatives were trained on correct phone techniques when they were hired. It was apparent that at least one representative had missed the training.

1. For each lettered item below that corresponds to a conversation excerpt above, briefly describe Craig's error(s) in phone technique.

    a. _____

    b. _____

    c. _____

    d. _____

    e. _____

    f. _____

    g. _____

2. For each lettered item below that corresponds to a conversation excerpt above, rephrase Craig's portion of the conversation to be more professional and courteous.

    a. _____

    b. _____

    c. _____

    d. _____

    e. _____

    f. _____

    g. _____

3. When Ariel schedules a training session for Craig, what aspects of answering incoming calls should be emphasized?

_____

_____

_____

CASE STUDY 3.2

The Case of the Automated Caller

Directions: *Analyze the situation below and then answer the questions that follow.*

Your phone rings, you have caller identification and recognize the number as your local bank. You pick up on the call only to find that it is an automated message announcing to you that your loan is past due by three days. You have been away on vacation and neglected to make the loan payment before you left. The message gives you a choice of options to speak with someone concerning how you wish to handle this situation. After listening to at least seven options, you decide to select the one that best fits your situation. You push that button only to find yet another automated message which is filled with more instructions and confusion. At this point you are about ready to hang up the phone when a "live" person comes on the line and asks if she can help you.

1. Do you think calling with an automated message on an overdue loan payment seems reasonable? Explain.

_____

_____

_____

2. What steps could the bank have taken in the way of calling you concerning your overdue loan payment?

_____

_____

_____

3. What parts of the message caused you the most confusion? Why?

_____

_____

_____

4. What steps would you take to correct this situation concerning automated phone calls?

_____

_____

_____

5. Have you personally ever experienced a similar type of automated phone call? If so, how have you handled it?

_____

_____

_____

Handling Special Types of Phone Calls

"There is always hope when people are forced to listen to both sides."
—*John Stuart Mill*

CHAPTER OBJECTIVES

Chapter 4 will help you:

1. Develop skill in handling special types of phone calls—requesting information, scheduling appointments, dealing with complaints, handling collections, and dealing with telemarketing.

2. Strengthen questioning and listening skills while handling special types of phone calls.

3. Demonstrate the importance of having easy access to information needed when handling a special type of call, which can save both time and money as well as promote goodwill.

PICTURE THIS

Today is the day that you have decided you will call the cable television provider to complain about a major problem with your cable. When you make the call, you get placed on hold. After 10 minutes of waiting, you learn that you need to have your account number before anyone can help you. You have to hang up and get back to the cable company shortly. While you are looking up your account number, the phone rings. You decide to let it ring and let the answering machine record the message. As it turns out, it is from your eye doctor reminding you of your upcoming appointment. It is a recorded message. Then, immediately following, the phone rings again. This time it is a telemarketer trying to sell you roofing. You are not interested in roofing, but somehow the telemarketer keeps you on the phone for at least 30 minutes. At this point you are very frustrated about all the calls and interruptions.

How could you have handled these special types of calls differently?

_____

_____

_____

_____

_____

■ REQUESTING INFORMATION

next slide

Phone calls *requesting information* involve both giving and receiving information. One of the most common reasons to use the phone is to request information.

Obtaining Information

Consider these questions BEFORE you make a call to obtain information:

1. **WHOM** are you calling?
2. **WHY** do you need the information?
3. **WHAT** information do you need?
4. **WHEN** do you need the information?
5. **HOW** will the information be used?

Additional important factors include:

next slide

- Timing of the call.
- Locating the correct phone number.
- Making the most efficient type of call.

Putting yourself in the place of the recipient will help you recognize that being professional and courteous is important.

When obtaining information, be *accurate* and *specific*. Putting yourself in the place of the recipient reinforces the importance of being professional and courteous.

FIGURE 4.1

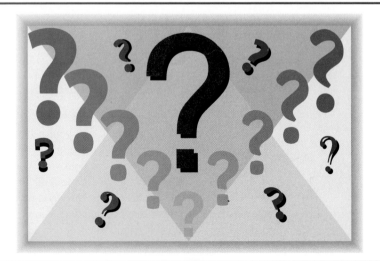

Placing Calls Requesting Information

When you are placing calls requesting information:

Be prepared to identify yourself professionally.   Identifying yourself professionally as you begin the conversation establishes good rapport.

> "Mr. Murphy, this is Anna Mason of Gruber Enterprises."

Establish whether the timing of your call is convenient.   Because you are requesting information, establishing whether this is a convenient time to call, is important. If the recipient feels a need to rush through your conversation because of another commitment, you may not get the recipient's full attention.

> "I would like additional information on the bid you submitted to us. Is this a convenient time to discuss the bid?"

Give the recipient time to respond while answering questions as completely as possible.   Allow the recipient to explain the answers to your questions. Likewise, answer questions of the recipient as completely as possible.

Confirm the information you have received during the call, and be sure to clarify questions or actions, if any, that need to be taken.

> "You'll deliver the revised bid to me next Wednesday."

Close the call courteously.   Thank the recipient for the information you received and close in a friendly and courteous tone.

> "I'll look forward to discussing the bid with you on Tuesday of next week, Mr. Murphy. Thank you. Good-bye."

ACTIVITY 4–1

Obtaining Information over the Phone

Purpose: To help you determine what questions should be asked when obtaining information via the phone. It will also help you understand that planning questions before you begin the call is an excellent idea and a time-saver.

Directions: *Read each scenario below, then write an appropriate response.*

1. Holly has decided that during her vacation she would like to visit her Aunt Justine, who lives in Fort Lauderdale, Florida. Holly, who lives in Omaha, Nebraska, wants to travel anytime between February 14 and April 15. She would like information from Central Airlines concerning schedules and prices. What information should Holly request when she calls Central Airlines?

    _____

    _____

    _____

    _____

    _____

_____

_____

_____

2. Kevin wants to purchase a new computer and printer. He plans to shop local stores and call out-of-state equipment centers that have a toll-free phone number. What information should Kevin request regarding complete computer packages when he calls the equipment centers?

_____

_____

_____

_____

_____

_____

_____

_____

3. Nicky has located three scholarships on the Internet for which she wants to apply. She has located contact numbers and wants to call for information. What questions should Nicky ask when she calls?

_____

_____

_____

_____

_____

_____

_____

_____

ACTIVITY 4-2

Expressing Your Needs Clearly

Purpose: To help you organize your thoughts before you speak in order to be clear.

Directions: _Read the statements below—some would be used to obtain information and others to provide information. Rewrite each statement to express the needs of the speaker._

1. I really think I want some information about the conference, but I am not sure where to start—with the dates, the time, the location, the cost, or what.

I am looking for information about the conference.
Could you provide me with the dates, time, location,
and cost of the upcoming conference.

2. Well . . . . I mean . . . . Oh gosh, I'm not sure of that date. I guess it is on Sunday at three, or maybe it is Tuesday at one. What should I do?

Is the date Sunday

What is the date of the event ?

_____

_____

3. Someone told us North Main Street. I think that's the street we are looking for, or maybe it's South Main Street. Maybe the street is spelled M-a-i-n-e or it could be M-a-i-n-n-e or M-a-i-n. I just don't know.

Is the location North or South Main Street ?

What is the correct spelling of Main ?

_____

_____

4. There was a young man here to see you at about 2 this afternoon. He had on a navy blue suit, I think. He said he was looking for a check you had for him. I can't remember his name, but he had a business card he gave me. I think he was the one who gave me that business card. Where is it?

_____

_____

_____

_____

5. Our Internet class will not be meeting next week, Jean. I think she said we would meet at four the following week in Room 210. Or was it at three in Room 110? I thought I wrote it down on a slip of paper. I guess it actually was at four in Room 110. Yes, I think that's when it was.

_____

_____

_____

_____

Providing Information

next slide

There will be numerous situations where you will be asked to provide information over the phone. While many types of information provided are of a repetitious nature and are handled by automated answering systems, there will be situations where you will be called upon to provide repetitious information and other specific information. In order to do this, you will need to be familiar with a wide variety of information related to the topic. Depending on the situation, you will also need to have access to written policies and procedures as they apply to the information you are providing. Always be prepared to respond to information requests in a positive, supportive, and respectful way.

Responding to a Call Requesting Information

When you are responding to callers requesting information:

Respond promptly. If you cannot answer the request immediately, tell the caller you will get back to them with the information as soon as possible in a positive, reassuring tone.

> "I will need to check on the status of your payment, Mrs. Rosberg. I will do that and get back to you later today. Does that work for you?"

Be helpful. Whenever you answer the phone, you represent yourself, and, if applicable, the business you work for. Your business relies on you to provide assistance to customers and the public. How you conduct yourself over the phone generates goodwill and possibly new business.

> "I would be happy to check on the status of your order, Mr. Carson."

Be accurate. Listen carefully to the caller's request for information and respond with accurate information. If you need to verify the information, follow up with the caller.

> "The service department has thoroughly checked your computer. They found that the problem was one of the print drivers."

Be complete. Ask relevant questions so that you can give complete information when you respond to the caller.

> "I have checked the latest catalogs for the phone equipment you specified. I am pleased to report that we can offer you several packages at very competitive prices."

Plan what you will do when you are not sure what to do. If you are not sure of what to do or say when someone is requesting information, put the caller on hold and ask your supervisor for help. If help is not available, tell the caller you will return the call to give an answer as soon as possible. Alternatively, you might want to transfer the caller to a person who can provide the requested information.

> "Unfortunately, I will not be able to give you an answer today, but I will get back to you within two days after I have done more research."

Say "no" in a positive manner. When you are not able to provide what the caller wants, be firm but courteous and professional.

> "It looks as if I will not be able to help you at this time but may be able to as soon as the new catalog arrives."

End the call courteously. Express appreciation for the call, whether or not you fulfilled the information request.

> "Thank you for calling, Ms. Weinsteger. I hope we can be of service to you again in the near future."

> "Thank you for calling, Mr. Henshaw. Perhaps we will be better able to help you next month, when our updated catalog arrives."

ASSESSMENT 4–1: ASSESS YOUR READINESS TO SCHEDULE APPOINTMENTS

Directions: *Read the statement below and assess your phone skill readiness to schedule appointments by marking one of the three choices. Be as honest as you can.*

	Always	Usually	Needs Work
1. Do I have scheduling materials in front of me before I begin to schedule an appointment?	____	____	____
2. Am I prepared to actively listen?	____	____	____
3. Do I have message forms available?	____	____	____
4. Do I offer creative alternatives when scheduling?	____	____	____
5. Do I verify all details of the scheduled appointment by repeating to the caller the day, date, and time of the appointment as well as caller's phone number?	____	____	____
6. Do I ask clarifying questions to avoid confusion?	____	____	____
7. Do I call and confirm the appointment the day before?	____	____	____
8. Am I thoroughly familiar with possible times I can schedule appointments?	____	____	____

Other comments concerning my phone skills when scheduling

appointments: _____

_____

_____

Phone skills on which I need to focus when scheduling

appointments: _____

_____

_____

_____

Analysis: If you marked "Always" to all statements, you have excellent phone skills when it comes to scheduling appointments.

If you marked "Usually" to all but one or two statements, you have very good phone skills when it comes to scheduling appointments.

If you marked "Always" or "Usually" to fewer than five statements, you have several areas you need to work on when it comes to scheduling appointments.

■ CALLS SCHEDULING APPOINTMENTS

Whether you are scheduling an appointment for yourself or someone else, you need to be very specific about your needs while applying all the important aspects of making a phone call covered earlier.

When you are scheduling appointments, keep in mind the following:

1. Have a calendar readily available to assist you. This may be an printed calendar or a hand-held electronic calendar. If you are scheduling appointments for several people, have their calendars readily available.

2. Once you have scheduled an appointment, be sure to verify the following information:

- Name of the patient, client, or customer.
- Exact address and phone number of the patient, client, or customer.
- Day, date, place, and time of appointment.
- Purpose of and/or other details of the appointment.
- Name of the person who made the appointment (if other than yourself).
- Identification of the caller including file number, account number, or case number (if appropriate, as in a doctor's, accountant's, or attorney's office).

Likewise, the caller needs to know the following information about the appointment:

- Name of person to be seen.
- Exact date and time of appointment.
- Location of appointment, with detailed directions.
- Special instructions.

Some offices that schedule appointments regularly call the patient, client, or customer one day before the appointment to confirm it either personally or by using an automated system. A missed appointment may result in a fee to the patient, client, or customer.

FIGURE 4.2

Never rely upon your memory—or force others to rely upon it—for details. Write appointment details on paper, or enter them in an electronic calendar.

ACTIVITY 4-3

Are These Scheduled Appointments Complete?

Purpose: To learn that scheduling appointments involves obtaining and recording complete information.

Directions: *Margaret wrote the following notes when scheduling appointments for her two managers, Sahana and Clay. Analyze the information given for each appointment to determine if it is complete. If the information is complete, write* OK *in the space provided; if it is not, indicate what is missing.*

1. For Sahana,

Marcia McNeil will see you concerning the service contract for equipment. Her number is 555-9080. The appointment is scheduled for Wednesday, March 14, at 11 A.M. in your office.

_____

_____

_____

2. For Clay,

    Bernice Kinney and Brooke Terrone will see you on March 13 at 9 A.M. I have scheduled Conference Room B for the meeting.

_____

_____

_____

3. For Clay,

    Peter Reardon will be in on Thursday, March 15, to see you.

_____

_____

4. For Sahana,

    Dewaine Craig and Nundi Romano are coming in for a one-hour appointment at 10 A.M. in your office. They want to discuss some marketing tips with you.

_____

_____

5. For Clay,

    Alesha Estes will be coming to meet with you at 2 P.M. on Monday, March 12. She wants to talk to you about planning a retirement party for a colleague. Her number is 201-555-8796.

_____

_____

■ HANDLING COMPLAINT CALLS

By its very nature, the word *complaint* denotes some type of problem and often causes people to react with negative feelings such as frustration, annoyance, or anger. Before you make a complaint call, you MUST get your own feelings under control to avoid further problems. Be sure you have the facts of the situation correct BEFORE you make a complaint call.

FIGURE 4.3 | Control Your Negative Feelings When Making a Complaint Call.

Making a Complaint Call

Remember these suggestions for expressing your needs when you have to make a complaint call.

Be courteous.   Do not demand to speak to the manager, accuse inappropriately, or imply that the listener cannot help you. Instead, describe the problem briefly and ask who can help you resolve it. Politeness will more likely result in an acceptable solution.

"This is Whitney Tulles. I would like to speak to someone about a shipment I received today."

Describe the error impersonally.   Use of the word you assigns blame for the error. Avoid using you by wording your remarks in the passive, not active, voice. Your goal is to keep the other person feeling positive and willing to help you.

Don't say: "You didn't send me the correct version of software!"

Do say: "It looks as if the wrong version of software was sent."

Suggest a solution that would be satisfactory to you.   Have a possible solution in mind. If your suggestion is reasonable, the other party may be more willing to consider it.

"Could you please send me the correct version of the software by overnight mail without extra charge. I need it tomorrow."

End the call courteously.   If you have been positive throughout the call, end the call courteously, making sure you thank the recipient.

"Thank you for your help. I'll look forward to receiving the correct software tomorrow morning."

ACTIVITY 4-4

Information Request and Complaint Calls

Purpose: To manage information request and complaint calls with professionalism and courtesy.

Directions: *The statements below are responses that a recipient gave to callers. Read each response. If the response was professional and courteous, write OK in the space provided. If it was not professional and courteous, rewrite the statement.*

1. Well, Mr. Chin, that is the way that meeting agenda has to be!

I'm sorry, Mr. Chin, but that agenda seems to work best for everyone.

2. Thank you for calling, Miss Bordeaux. I will be in touch with you soon.

OK

_____

_____

_____

3. The advertising campaign will not be changed. That involves too much work to rearrange everything at this late time in the marketing season.

Unfortunately, it is too late in the marketing season to change the advertising campaign.

4. I am sorry that we had you scheduled on the wrong flight. I can arrange for you to be picked up at the airport by one of our representatives. Would that help you?

OK

_____

_____

_____

5. We can provide that information. However, I must warn you that it will cost you quite a bit of money, because you know our time is valuable and it will take a lot of time to research our database.

We can provide that info; however there is an extra charge.

6. I will be glad to send that book right out to you if you will provide me with the necessary information.

OK

_____

_____

_____

7. The meeting will not be taking place. You can call to find out when it will be rescheduled; we can't afford to call you.

Please call us to find out when the meeting will take place.

8. The items you are requesting were delivered to our warehouse last Thursday, but we haven't had time to inventory them yet. What do you expect of us?

The items were delivered last Thursday. Once they have been inventoried, we will give you a call.

9. I expect to have that answer within the hour. I will be glad to call and leave a message on your voice mail, if you wish.

OK _____

_____

_____

10. I don't understand why you are upset. Why couldn't you call us? We have had so many applications to process that we certainly can't call everyone!

Because of the number of applications, we are unable to call everyone.

_____

Responding to Complaints

Unfortunately, many people voice complaints in negative ways over the phone. Such experiences can cause you to lose control and react angrily to the caller. Applying the following important points will help you manage these complaint calls:

Managing Complaint Calls

next slide

Answer the phone promptly and identify yourself properly.   Answer the phone in a pleasant, helpful manner. Identify yourself appropriately and offer to assist the caller.

> "Superintendent's office; this is Nikki. How may I help you?"

Ask open-ended questions.   Be respectful of the caller's feelings, but try to maintain control of the conversation. Redirect the caller's attention from feelings to the facts of the situation. Ask open-ended questions to help you determine the nature of the problem.

> "What is the nature of the defect?"

Confirm your understanding of the problem.   An emotional caller can confuse the facts, making it difficult for you to understand the situation. If necessary, politely ask the caller to repeat the problem. Once you think you understand the facts, confirm them with the caller to make sure that you both understand the problem.

> "Okay, Mrs. Norton, let me be sure I understand the problem. You ordered one headboard in antique blue, and you received one headboard in antique brown. Is that correct?"

Be helpful and offer solutions.   If it is clear that you or your company is in error, apologize for the error and the inconvenience it caused. If you can, offer a solution to the caller's problem or agree to a solution that is reasonable.

End the call courteously and positively.   Leave the caller feeling positive about you, your company, and the results of the call.

■ MAKING COLLECTION CALLS

In a **collection call,** the caller's goal is to collect money for an account balance by getting a commitment from the recipient to pay. Collection agencies train employees how to make collection calls. You still may have to make collection calls on your own for personal business matters. If you are placed in such a position, keep these important points in mind.

Collecting money for overdue payments can disturb the recipient. Treat the recipient respectfully and courteously.

Making Collection Calls

Use these guidelines when making collection calls.

Identify yourself properly and establish the convenience of the call.   Be positive, especially when collecting money over the phone. The call will not be pleasant to the recipient, so be sure that the recipient has time to speak with you. Be aware that some recipients may know what the call is about and put off talking to you.

> "Hello, Mr. Chin. This is Heidi from the Cornish Water Co. Is this a good time to speak with you?"

State your purpose clearly and directly.   Be direct to maintain control of the conversation.

> "I am calling about your account balance with us."

> "I am calling about your past-due account balance."

Listen to the recipient's response.   Allow the recipient to explain the delay involving the account payment. Take precise notes.

Request prompt action on the part of the recipient.   Get a commitment regarding payment from the recipient. Whenever possible, request payment in terms of the needs, interests, and pride of the recipient.

> "Can you make a partial payment now and send the remaining balance within thirty days?"

> "You've always paid on time in the past. How soon do you expect to be able to clear your present balance?"

End the call courteously, repeating the action to be taken by the recipient. Thank the recipient and repeat the payment arrangement for clarification.

> "Thank you, Mr. Chin. We'll look forward to receiving your check for $500 before July 1. Good-bye."

Record your conversation so that you can follow up after a reasonable amount of time has elapsed.   Document conversation to provide proof of discussions and outline possible future actions.

ACTIVITY 4-5

How Would You Handle These Collection Call Scenarios?

Purpose: To give you practice in considering and learning how you might handle three different types of collection call scenarios.

Scenario 1   The person who regularly makes collection calls on behalf of the Yorktowne Community Credit Union is on extended sick leave. No collections calls have been made on behalf of outstanding loan payments for nearly three months. Your manager announces to you when you arrive at work that you will be handling some collection calls for the next few days. Your training in phone collection is limited.

How will you handle this assignment? Be as specific as possible with justification for your reasoning.

_____

_____

_____

_____

_____

Scenario 2   For the past month you have volunteered over 10 hours to collect money on behalf of your local public television station. During that time you were able to generate over 50 new memberships with quite a large sum of money in pledges. Unfortunately, not everyone has paid even a portion of their pledge. There are three in particular that pledged $500 each that have not sent in their checks. They did not want to use their credit cards. So, you are calling them shortly to try to collect the pledge.

How will you begin the collection call for this scenario?

_____

_____

What specific questions might you ask?

_____

_____

What is your plan if the customer is reacting negatively?

_____

_____

Scenario 3   You have a lawn care business with over 35 customers. Most of the customers pay by cash or check when you finish the lawn care work. There is one customer, Mr. Tauroney, who ALWAYS follows you around whenever you are mowing his lawn. He is very fussy and unfriendly, and you find that you are spending more time than necessary at his home. He never pays you when the work is completed. He always wants you to send him a bill, which you have done three times already. He has not paid his bill. Today you are in the process of going over your outstanding accounts, and Mr. Tauroney's tops the list. You decide that you will give him a call to try to collect the money.

What materials will you need to have in front of you before you make the call to Mr. Tauroney?

_____

_____

How do you plan to approach the conversation with Mr. Tauroney to make it as positive an experience as possible?

_____

_____

_____

■ TELEMARKETING CALLS

Marketing or selling a product or service using a phone is called *telemarketing* and is widely used today as an efficient and cost-effective way to sell a wide variety of products and services. *Telemarketing* is generally used for the following reasons:

- Selling by targeting leads.
- Reaching a wider range of potential customers.
- Using time more efficiently.
- Obtaining feedback quickly.

Telemarketers must possess a number of extremely important skills to be successful. These include:

next slide

1. Thorough knowledge about the product or service being marketed.
2. Excellent oral communication skills including fine-tuned listening skills.
3. A positive attitude as demonstrated by a pleasant voice and persistent but not an overly aggressive style of communication.

Telemarketers often work for companies that provide telemarketing services for one or more clients. Telemarketers are carefully trained to target the service or product being sold. They usually operate with a script and carefully controlled procedure, thus obtaining the maximum benefit from all calls made.

Some of the more common uses of telemarketing include the following:

- Targeting sales leads
- Reaching customers worldwide
- Using time in the selling process more effectively
- Obtaining instant feedback on products or services

The Telemarketing Setting

next slide

In addition to the already discussed positive setting for making any phone call, there are several very important factors that promote a positive environment for selling via the phone:

- **A well-ventilated and temperature-controlled environment.** Attempting to sell anything via the phone in a room that is too hot or too cold adversely affects an individual's success in selling.

- **An ergonomic environment.** Work space should be adequate in size and essential furniture should be provided that best fits the person making calls. This includes a desk, chair, and computer properly positioned for maximum performance and use. Most telemarketers use headsets that free up their hands for keying and any manual note taking. Lighting should also be adequate and steps taken to prevent intrusion of unwanted sound and interruptions.

- **Use of current phone technology.** The phone system used should be personalized to meet the needs of the telemarketer for optimum performance. Specific training should be ongoing for using phone technology.

- **Support.** A telemarketer must be supported by a manager who is easily accessible whenever needed.

Making the Telemarketing Call

As was previously mentioned, for a telemarketer ongoing, specific training is essential for success. A successful telemarketer can do well financially by working hard to develop customers. It all hangs on "making that call" properly.

Most telemarketers are provided with a database of potential clients from which to begin, but in addition a telemarketer MUST develop techniques for acquiring new customers. Before you make your call, consider these thoughts:

- **Be aware of time.** A great deal of time can be wasted if you are not aware of the time. Many telemarketing systems today are built in with timing devices to monitor time spent on calls. If not, use a clock or timer to help you monitor your time.

- **Put a smile on your face.** Smiling loosens your vocal chords and creates a more relaxed feeling in the tone of your voice.

- **Be sure to follow up calls.** Some calls by their very nature necessitate your conducting a follow-up call to further clarify a potential sale. Use technology to assist you in following up any potential sales—and be certain you follow through on them!

Making a Telemarketing Call

Follow these guidelines when making a telemarketing call.

Be sure you reach the right person.   As the telemarketer, you may reach a receptionist who screens calls. Your goal is to be forwarded to the potential customer or client. Be self-confident and courteous.

Receptionist: "Good afternoon, Dearborn Office Center. May I help you?"

Telemarketer: "Yes, hopefully you can. This is Myra Burbank calling from Park Associates in San Francisco. May I speak with Dean Perry?"

Receptionist: "I'm sorry. Mr. Perry is not available at the moment. Could someone else help you?"

Telemarketer: "Perhaps. I'm following up on a previous call to Mr. Perry about his interest in several new office chairs."

Receptionist: "Perhaps Ms. Chan could help you; she handles equipment purchases. Would you like to speak with her?"

Telemarketer: "That would be fine. Thank you."

The telemarketer was polite at all times, even when she was told Mr. Perry was unavailable. She succeeded in being forwarded to someone who might have the authority to make purchases.

Generate interest.   At the beginning of the call, tell the prospect the reason for your call. Indicate possible benefits of listening to your message. You may mention a mutual acquaintance who provided the prospect's name. Ask a few questions to determine if the prospect is interested.

Telemarketer: "Ms. Hunter, this is Tim Spisak. Your name was given to me by Constance Long. She thought you might be interested in hearing more about a new type of interactive advertising software we are selling. She mentioned that you have your own home-based consulting business where you are in the process of building a client base. Is that true?"

Ms. Hunter: "Yes, I do have my own business here in my home, and I am interested."

Telemarketer: "Well, if you could spare about five minutes, I'd like to explain how this interactive advertising software can help you."

Ms. Hunter: "Fine, as long as it's only five minutes. I have a meeting to go to in ten minutes."

If Ms. Hunter had indicated she was not interested, the telemarketer could have asked two or three more questions to generate interest. If there still was no interest, the call would be ended. Since Ms. Hunter indicated that she was interested, the telemarketer presented the product.

Make the sales presentation.   Once the prospect is interested, and he or she has given the time to talk with you, describe the product or service. Tell the prospect about one or two major benefits he or she would enjoy about your product or service.

Overcome objections.   As a telemarketer, you can expect potential customers to raise objections to the sales presentation. You may plan your responses ahead of time, usually using a prepared script. If you cannot overcome the prospect's objections, or if for each objection you overcome, the prospect thinks of another, thank the prospect for speaking with you and end the call.

Secure the sale.   If you overcome the objections raised by the potential customer, ask for the order immediately. One way to do this is to ask a forced-choice question.

"Would you prefer to order the oak or cherry desk?"

Confirm the order.   If the customer agreed to purchase your product or service, verify the name, address, payment information, and the details of the order. Read this information back to the customer.

End the call courteously.   End the call courteously, thanking the customer and saying good-bye.

SUMMARY

1. One of the most common reasons to use the phone is to request information.

2. Be accurate and specific in what you request.

3. Determine what information is being requested so you can quickly and efficiently process the call.

4. When scheduling appointments, have a calendar before you to assist to dates and times.

5. A complaint call can present many challenges because it involves some type of problem or mistake.

6. Get negative feelings in check before making a complaint call.

7. Be positive, especially when collecting money over the phone.

8. Telemarketing is the most popular way to market and sell a wide variety of products and services today because it is efficient and cost-effective.

9. Telemarketers must have excellent oral communication skills, quick decision-making abilities, and strong listening skills. They must reflect a positive attitude, have a pleasant voice, and be persistent but not overly aggressive.

■ APPLICATION ACTIVITY 4–1

Practicing Positive Responses

Directions: *Read each of the following responses from a phone conversation. Determine if each is positive and courteous. If it is, place a check mark in the* Yes *column. If it is not, place a check mark in the* No *column. Then rewrite the response to make it positive.*

	Yes	No
1. "I sent you my bill over five weeks ago, and you still haven't sent me a check yet."	_____	_____
2. "It would be extremely helpful if you would provide me with that information."	_____	_____
3. "McDonald & Martin, Sarah here. Hold on."	_____	_____
4. "You must have asked for the hooded sweatshirt. It says so right here on my copy of the order."	_____	_____
5. "I don't have time to check that right now."	_____	_____
6. "Thank you for calling, Mrs. Rankin. We appreciate your bringing that problem to our attention."	_____	_____
7. "The Telecommunications Department must have made another mistake. Hold on, I'll transfer you."	_____	_____

8. "I don't know what you are talking about."   _____   _____

   _____

   _____

   _____

9. "That's not my job."   _____   _____

   _____

   _____

   _____

10. "I'm not interested in having it fixed!
    I want a new one."   _____   _____

   _____

   _____

   _____

APPLICATION ACTIVITY 4–2

What Messages Do Pictures Convey in Handling Special Types of Phone Calls?

Purpose: To gain greater insight into the role physical and verbal behavior play in handling special types of phone calls.

Directions: *Use the Internet to search for pictures of individuals using a phone. Select three pictures that you feel represent the following:*

a. Frustration in making a complaint call

b. Satisfaction in scheduling an appointment

c. Assertiveness in dealing with a telemarketer

Once you have obtained the pictures, write two or three paragraphs reflecting your thoughts and feelings about the pictures, especially with how completing an activity such as this will help you when you are faced with a similar type of call. Share your thoughts with your classmates.

_____

_____

_____

_____

_____

_____

_____

_____

_____

_____

_____

_____

_____

_____

_____

_____

_____

_____

_____

_____

_____

_____

_____

_____

CASE STUDY 4.1

The Inexperienced Telemarketer

Directions: *Analyze the situation described below and then answer the questions that follow. Try to provide answer that reflect your understanding of the concepts you learned in Chapter 4.*

Ryan Keelman has been hired to telemarket advertising space in a new weekly community newspaper. Ryan's previous telemarketing experience was with a large marketing firm. That experience covered all aspects of the marketing process, including prospects, scripts, product information, and procedures.

The newspaper hopes that with Ryan's experience, he should be able to start selling right away. Ryan feels a great deal of pressure, so he picks up the local *Yellow Pages* and immediately starts making calls. The first day presents many challenges. First, he selects businesses to call that rarely advertise in the local paper. Second, when he does reach someone who might be interested, he doesn't have enough information to answer questions. Third, he can't think of reasons why the prospect should advertise with the paper he represents rather than the established competitor. As a result, he makes only one minor sale that day.

The next day Ryan arrives at work and realizes he has to plan before making any calls.

1. Why is Ryan having difficulty reaching appropriate prospects when he makes calls randomly?

   _____

   _____

   _____

   _____

2. How could a telemarketing script help Ryan manage his telemarketing calls?

   _____

   _____

   _____

   _____

3. What information should be contained in a telemarketing script to help Ryan during his calls?

   _____

   _____

   _____

   _____

CASE STUDY 4.2

A Rapidly Developing Scheduling Situation at Limington Rapids Total Body Care Center!

Directions: *Analyze the situation described below and answer the questions that follow. Try to provide answers that reflect your understanding of the concepts you have studied in Chapter 4.*

Nicole and Cheryl both work Monday–Friday at Limington Rapids Total Body Care Center. In addition, Sherri and Nike also work there Tuesday–Thursday. Each has her own appointment book, with Nicole and Cheryl keeping their appointments on their personal hand-held calendars.

Very recently, Cheryl broke her right wrist playing volleyball at a family reunion. She will not be able to be a stylist for at least 10 weeks, but she has agreed to schedule appointments during this time. Nicole has agreed to take Cheryl's regular appointments during that time.

Limington Rapids Total Body Care Center has automated appointment reminder software, which Cheryl is trying to use with one hand. She is quite confident that she got most of the customers in on the first try.

Nicole does not feel as comfortable with the software and prefers to call her customers personally to verify their appointments. This takes a great deal of time, but she believes in the "personal touch" when scheduling appointments.

Sherri and Nike just rely on what they schedule in their appointment books opting not to make calls or use the automated equipment.

One Thursday in the early afternoon, the shop begins to fill up with people. Only a handful were using the tanning booths. Cheryl is sitting at the receptionist desk. Within one hour at least 10 people had arrived, all claiming that Cheryl was to do their hair or give them a manicure. Nicole goes into a panic! Sherri is not working and Nike needs to get home because of babysitter problems. As Cheryl begins to have a conversation with all the customers, she soon realizes that she made a major error—she rescheduled two days worth of customers on one day. Oops!

1. What should Cheryl do?

   _____

   _____

   _____

   _____

2. How would you prevent this from happening in the future?

   _____

   _____

   _____

   _____

3. How could an appointment book and automated software be put to better use at Limington Rapids Total Body Care Center?

_____

_____

_____

_____

4. What other advice would you offer Cheryl, Nicole, Sherri, and Nike?

_____

_____

_____

_____

Servicing the Customer on the Phone

"Manners are the happy way of doing things."
—Ralph Waldo Emerson

CHAPTER OBJECTIVES

Chapter 5 will help you:

1. Establish a level of exemplary service with the customer when using a phone.

2. Use the phone effectively to service customers.

3. Focus on the importance your voice plays in servicing customers professionally.

4. Strengthen your listening skills whenever you are servicing customers.

5. Use effective questioning when servicing the customer.

6. Integrate technology when servicing the customer in order to save time and money.

PICTURE THIS

As the person designated to do ordering for your small business handling bedding and supplies for cleaning, you recognize that you need to order new bedding. You remember ordering over the phone at the L. L. Stolt Company a few months ago. The bedding was wonderfully durable, and you have decided to go with them again. You have their toll-free number and decide to call to place an order. You pick up the phone and call. You immediately get a choice of options. You choose the option for ordering and are placed on hold with intermittent messages that your call is important and it will not be long now. Finally, someone comes on the line to take your order. When the customer service representative starts questioning you, you recognize that you are in trouble. You don't remember the style, the size, the color, and how many you need. The customer service representative starts questioning you in a very calm manner at first, but then you get the feeling things are beginning to escalate in that you can't answer any of the questions. Finally, you just say, "I'll call back later, good-bye."

How would you handle this situation?

_____

_____

_____

_____

ASSESSMENT 5-1: ASSESS YOUR CUSTOMER SERVICE PHONE SKILLS

Directions: *Read the statement below and assess your customer service phone skills by placing a check mark next to each statement that applies to your personal customer service phone skills.*

_____   **1.** My voice has a pleasant pitch and tone that is not offensive.

_____   **2.** I have all the necessary information in front of me for handling the call.

_____   **3.** I establish proper identification whether making or receiving a customer service phone call.

_____   **4.** I always try to listen attentively while responding in a positive and professional manner.

_____   **5.** I articulate dialects and accents clearly and accurately.

_____   **6.** My voice is often either too loud or too soft, depending on my mood.

_____   **7.** I always try to smile when I am speaking on the phone, which loosens my vocal chords and creates a friendlier and more relaxing style of communicating with the customer.

_____   **8.** I try to not speak too loudly or too fast to customers.

_____   **9.** I tend to pause too much when I am speaking.

_____   **10.** I have a plan in place to overcome customer objections when I am servicing customers.

Analysis: If you checked most of the statements, you have **excellent** customer service phone skills.

If you checked all but one or two, you have **very good** customer service phone skills.

If you checked only one or two, you definitely need to work on **improving** your customer service phone skills.

■ SERVICING CUSTOMERS—WHAT'S IT ALL ABOUT?

By definition, ***customer service*** involves all aspects of servicing customers' needs, including answering questions, dealing with complaints, or fielding any other concerns related to customer needs.

Because of the convenience, customer service is handled over the phone instead of face-to-face. These calls are managed by ***customer service representatives,*** commonly known as ***CSRs.***

Providing and practicing efficient and positive ***customer service*** is a highly desirable quality when doing business—whatever the size or situation. Businesses that practice poor quality customer service often lose clients permanently. Learning to value and respect your customer's needs goes a long way in establishing and perpetuating continued goodwill as well as continuing to develop a potential customer.

What causes poor customer service? The major reasons include:

- Lack of interest in the customer's individual needs.
- Poor decision-making skill.
- Use of ineffective communication skills with a customer.
- Inadequate customer service training.

How do you provide quality customer service in order to retain customers and build potential customers?

Your Voice Quality

Use your voice to convey a positive message to the customer.

The quality of your voice is extremely important when practicing customer service. Your voice can convey messages by its pitch, tone, and speed, thus creating a picture of yourself. If you are servicing customers with dialects or accents, the way you speak can make the difference in communicating positively or negatively. Think about how your phone personality translates to a customer who is unhappy or to someone who is trying to obtain information.

FIGURE 5.1 | The Tone of Voice You Use in a Conversation Has More Effect than the Actual Words.

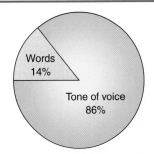

Maintaining Voice Quality

Keep the following points in mind to help you maintain your voice quality on the phone:

Maintain a tone that is positive, clear, and enthusiastic.   This makes the customer interested.

Create comfortable conversation.   Customer service professionals, or representatives, often use scripts that help them to create a positive voice quality.

Use a vocabulary that is easy to understand.   This creates a relaxed, positive atmosphere. The way you emphasize certain words can contribute to delivering quality customer service, instead of poor customer service.

Keep a smile on your face.   In fact, check your smile in a mirror periodically to remind you how important it is!

ACTIVITY 5–1

Using the Right Words with Customers

Purpose: To help you understand how your voice can emphasize certain words, changing a customer's perception positively or negatively.

Directions: *Read each sentence below—if possible, with a partner. Emphasize with your voice the words in bold print. (Notice that each sentence is identical, with different words being emphasized.) Write a comment about each sentence, giving your reaction to the words being emphasized and the different effects each phrase has in relation to practicing good customer service.*

1. **How** may I help you?

2. How may I **help** you?

_____

_____

_____

3. **Unfortunately,** our supply of that item is totally exhausted.

4. Unfortunately, our supply of that item is **totally** exhausted.

_____

_____

_____

5. What is the **best** time to return your call?

6. What is the best time to **return** your call?

_____

_____

_____

7. **Thank you** for that information; I will get back to you shortly.

8. Thank you for that information; I will get **back** to you shortly.

_____

_____

_____

9. Let's **verify** that date—that's Monday, November 23.

10. Let's verify that date—that's **Monday, November 23.**

_____

_____

_____

Establishing Proper Identification   When you try to reach a specific person, you may encounter special challenges. For example:

Professional: "Is this the home of Donna Moreau?"

Recipient: "Yes, it is."

Professional: "May I please speak with her?"

Recipient: "I'm sorry, Donna is not here right now. Could you speak with someone else or could I take a message?"

Professional: "No, I will call again. Thank you."

In the preceding example, the caller wanted to contact a **specific** person but was unsuccessful in doing so. You may not always reach the correct person in each call. Be polite to the person who answers the phone to help ensure the success of future calls made to that business or residence.

In the following conversation, the representative does reach the customer.

Professional: "Good morning. May I speak to Sherrillyn Cardoza?"

Recipient: "This is Sherrillyn Cardoza."

Professional: "Sherrillyn, how are you? This is Michael from the Frame Factory. I am calling concerning your problem with a frame we made for you. Is this a good time to speak with you?"

The caller established proper identification with the recipient. The caller was polite, the recipient knew the purpose of the call, and the caller established the convenience of the call.

ACTIVITY 5-2

How's the Customer Service?

Purpose: To learn to make and receive customer service calls professionally.

Directions: _Read each scenario below, analyzing each for correct procedure concerning answering and making calls. Then respond to the questions._

Scenario 1   The All Points South Travel Agency in Salt Lake City, Utah, has expanded to include a subdivision dealing with international travel. All agents have been assigned specific areas to cover. The phone rings, and Jon picks up the phone. The customer is interested in booking a trip to the New England area. Jon knows the customer and would like to help her, but he knows he has been assigned a new area. Jon tells the customer, "Mrs. Valentina, I no longer schedule trips within the United States. However, I will be happy to transfer your call to the correct department if you will please hold."

1. a. Is Jon practicing good phone procedure?

_____ Yes   _____ No

b. Comments:

_____

_____

_____

Scenario 2   Marilee is trying to contact the Director of Admissions at San Anselmo College. The receptionist answers the phone by saying, "San Anselmo College, may I help you?"

Marilee states that she would like to speak to the Director of Admissions.

The receptionist asks, "Who is calling?" After Marilee states her name, the receptionist replies, "I am sorry, the director is not in today. Do you want to leave a message?"

2. a. Is the receptionist practicing good phone customer service?

_____ Yes   _____ No

b. Comments:

_____

_____

_____

Scenario 3   Anna is just finishing up her weekly report on customer service calls. Her phone is ringing repeatedly. After about eight rings, she answers it, "Hello!"

It is a customer who is calling concerning a problem with a rental car.

Anna is extremely frustrated and replies, "I'm sorry. I can't speak with you just now. Could you call back Monday?"

3. a. How would you rate Anna's customer service over the phone ?

_____ Acceptable   _____ Unacceptable

b. Comments:

_____

_____

_____

Answering Techniques

If you are answering the phone, as opposed to making the call, keep the following points in mind.

1. **Answer the phone on the first or second ring.** If the phone continues to ring, the caller will not appreciate your lateness and could feel neglected.

2. **Provide your name and any other appropriate identification.** The identification may include your department, division, or unit.

   "Customer Service; this is Jane. How may I help you?"

   "Book Department. Mrs. Drinkwater speaking."

3. **Smile when you answer the phone.** A smile relaxes your vocal chords. You might want to put a sign with the word "smile" on it near your phone as a reminder.

Smile when talking on the phone. It makes your voice sound pleasant.

Listening Actively   Active listening is important to communicating effectively with customers. Many of the listening concepts you learned in Chapter 1 also apply to customer service. Several other considerations are directly targeted at customer service calls. When you talk with customers, listen to their needs. Do not immediately launch into the conversation.

Listening Actively

Keep the following points in mind to listen actively when providing quality customer service.

Listen carefully to the concerns and needs of customers. Are they angry or are they simply clarifying a point?

Determine what your reaction will be to the situation. Remember, the customer is always right—whether or not that is true!

Indicate your willingness to listen to the needs of your customer. Use reinforcing words, such as "I see" or "I understand." This will let your customer know that you are concerned and are listening.

Record the major points of the discussion with customers. Documentation is important. It can help you assess the situation, repeat concerns, or determine what action will please the customer.

Remember, listening is a skill that must be practiced constantly. Eliminate poor listening habits so that you can serve your customer efficiently and effectively.

Asking Questions   Ask the right questions to carry out customer service effectively. Expert customer service centers around questions. The questions should help you provide service for your customers with a personal, helpful style.

Background questions help you to direct your caller to the correct department or person, or to obtain important information to serve the customer.

> "I see, Mr. Martin. Will you please answer several questions so I can try to handle your problem immediately."

The open question, as described in Chapter 1, requires more of an answer than *yes* or *no*. Use the open question to help you explore the problem the customer is having, to identify major issues, and to determine possible solutions.

> "Could you explain the situation to me, please?"

> "What do you think should be your next course of action?"

The *verification question,* or confirmation question, verifies or confirms that information provided is correct or understood.

> "How do you feel about trying that approach?"

> "May I assume, then, that you are willing to go along with that for the moment?"

ACTIVITY 5-3

Listening to Your Customers' Needs

Purpose: To learn to listen to your customers' needs. Customers are not always direct in stating their needs. Sometimes you need to get more information from them before you can help them.

Directions: *Read each statement below to understand what the customer needs. If you understood the customer's needs, place a check mark in the Yes column. If you did not understand the customer's needs, place a check mark in the No column. Then explain specifically your reason for not understanding.*

	Yes	No
1. Your customer screamed at you over the phone about how uneducated the staff must be in your company.	_____	_____
2. Your customer was polite, friendly, and knew that she wanted the yellow drape to be replaced with a blue drape, No. 793GA, of the same size.	_____	_____

3. When your customer indicated some
    negativism concerning your promotion, you
    replied in a pleasant manner, trying a positive
    approach.

    _____

    _____

    _____

4. Your customer spoke to you in garbled tones,
    as if she had something in her mouth. You
    could hear a lot of background music and
    other noise.

    _____

    _____

    _____

■ USING THE RIGHT TECHNOLOGY FOR EFFICIENT CUSTOMER SERVICE

Utilizing technology to assist you in better servicing customers can pay big dividends in both time and money. Knowing which technology works best for you in your situation is very important. Some businesses rely completely on automated answering services with highly sophisticated voice-activated responses as a part of their customer services. Others have less sophisticated messages recorded to assist in servicing customers.

Voice Mail, Answering Machines, and Pagers

Leaving messages via voice mail, answering machines, and pagers creates a gap between you and the customer. There is no doubt that when a customer has to leave a message, the feeling of the "personal touch" is gone. It can be a positive experience in that it clearly sends a message that someone is AWARE of your needs as a customer and is taking a positive action to keep you as a customer.

Some customer service numbers connect the customer to a recording that may offer a selection of several options. Other customer service recordings have an option that bypasses the message and allows the caller to speak to a person. Customers can become frustrated quickly when they reach a recorded message and are forced to make several selections and perhaps never speak to an actual person.

Pagers, beepers, and ***cell phones*** are small, portable devices that beep or vibrate to let you know that someone has called you. These portable devices may be carried or worn, such as in a bag or on a belt. They can improve customer service greatly because they instantly notify the user of a call. Usually

Answering devices can increase productivity and serve customers better if customer service representatives return calls to customers who have left messages.

these devices work only within a certain geographic range unless additional options are provided.

■ TIPS FOR MORE EFFECTIVE USE OF VOICE MAIL, ANSWERING MACHINES, AND PAGERS

- Whenever you leave a message, be sure you speak clearly and intelligently. When you record or leave a message on any answering device, enunciate your words and form a clear message.

  "This is Sam Bright of Bright Enterprises. Please call me at 614-555-7824 on Tuesday, June 3, between 8 A.M. and 1 P.M. about the amendment to the Brigson contract."

- Be sure you repeat and spell out any unique names or words that would be confusing. It is always a good idea to repeat a call back number as well for additional clarity.

  "This is Felicia Macksell calling—that's F-e-l-i-c-i-a M-a-c-k-s-e-l-l. My number is 207-555-3409."

- Avoid unusual noises in the background such as music or other distracting sounds. This can cause additional confusion and miscommunication.

- ALWAYS include your name, number, and time you called whenever you are leaving a message. This will serve to avoid any confusion.

- Establish a plan for using your pager that works efficiently and is considerate of those around you. Carry your pager with you at all times with easy access, such as clipped to a belt or other piece of clothing that works best for you. It will be difficult to communicate with you if your pager is left elsewhere. You may be able to reach pager users at certain times of the day only. Know what circumstances require you to page the user, for example, emergency situations or when the individual is in a certain location.

- Avoid running to the phone when your pager goes off. You will need to determine the importance of the caller on the pager.

- Turn off your pager or other device when you are in a public place where a pager going off would be an interruption such as in a restaurant or movie theater. If you must leave your pager turned on in this environment, try to sit in a location where its noise would cause the least interference.

- Change your voice mail, answering machine, or pager message periodically to keep the information current. Record professional messages that are current and meet customers' needs.

  "Hello, you have reached Gerald Harkins of Dearborn Communications. If you are calling from the western territory, please contact Angela Lytle at 609-555-7888; I no longer service that area. If you are calling from the southeastern territory, please leave your name, phone number, and a brief message. I will be glad to return your call as soon as possible."

- Write your message for incoming calls BEFORE recording it. Write your message that will answer incoming calls. Review it for clarity before you record it.

"You have reached Elizabeth Mazzaro of A-1 Engineering. I am out of the office from May 11–14 and will be returning on May 15. Please leave your name, phone number, and a brief message so that I may return your call. Thank you."

ACTIVITY 5-4

Leaving Messages for Customers

Purpose: To help you learn whether it is appropriate to leave a message for the customer.

Directions: *Read each statement below and determine whether a message should be left for the customer. If a message should be left, place a check mark in the "Yes" column. If a message should not be left, place a check mark in the "No" column. Explain your answers.*

	Yes	No
1. You want to tell a potential customer about the services of your advertising company. You hope he might be interested.	____	____
2. You are returning a call to one of your customers who called you earlier today. She is having a problem with the new printer she purchased recently from your company.	____	____
3. You are finishing up a sales campaign. The person you are calling bought a lot of office supplies from you during another sales campaign. You feel strongly that he might be interested in doing so again. The sales campaign will end in three days.	____	____

4.   You want one of your regular customers to
     call you today to finalize an order that needs to
     be processed by the end of the day.   _____   _____

     _____

     _____

     _____

     _____

5.   You have previously called this potential
     customer and left a message, but no one ever
     returned your call. You know this customer is
     very interested in your products. You have
     information about a special offer that you feel
     this person could take advantage of.   _____   _____

     _____

     _____

     _____

     _____

     _____

■ SERVICING CUSTOMERS WHILE USING THE INTERNET

Online customer service is used extensively in today's electronic world of
communication. The Internet is used to answer questions, sell products, and
follow up with customers after purchases are made. This topic will be covered in greater detail in Chapter 6.

FIGURE 5.2 |

Some Companies Pro-
vide Customer Service
Options on Internet
Home Pages.

The **Internet** is a worldwide
collection of computer
networks that are
electronically connected to
permit communication and
the exchange of information.
Databases, libraries, and
other information sources
are available for thousands
of topics ranging from simple
to complex.

World Wide Web
(also referred to as **The Web**
or **WWW**) is a place on the
Internet where documents
and information are stored
for use. Web pages use
graphics and text to show
information about topics.

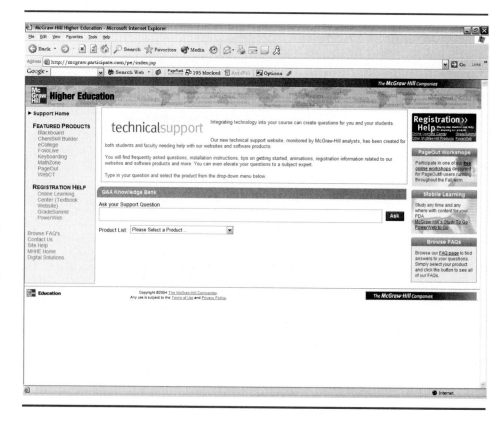

■ UNDERSTANDING CUSTOMER NEEDS

All customers have basic needs that you must be prepared to meet as a customer service professional.

- They need to be treated pleasantly.
- They need to be treated professionally throughout the entire call.
- They need to be offered possible solutions to their problems or concerns.

Reading Your Customer's Mind

With customer service training and some experience, you will learn to "read" your customer's mind. You will find that most customers want to be treated fairly and professionally whatever the situation. Often you will be able to predict the outcome that the customer wants.

Customers do not like to fill out extensive surveys and write long answers. Similarly, they do not like to provide long answers or explanations over the phone. In both situations, customers respond well to questions that are direct and require a simple answer.

Dealing with Objections

Ideally, all customer service calls would yield positive responses. Realistically, objections do occur, and sometimes the caller is not interested in responding positively to a customer service representative. When a customer raises an objection, you must handle the situation quickly and effectively. If you do not, you could lose a customer or a potential customer.

Listening is the key to managing objections. You must understand what you are hearing from your customer and know what you can say to help overcome the objection.

Dealing with Customer Objections

Keep these points in mind as you deal with customer objections.

Control your emotions.   Perhaps there is a reason why the customer is demonstrating a particular emotion. Listen to the customer carefully, and keep your emotions under control.

Determine what is the major objection, and deal with that particular one.   Use good questioning techniques to help you manage the call and establish good customer service.

Reply to the customer in a positive tone, and respond only to the specific objection.   Do not waiver from the discussion.

Offer possible solutions.   Try to work out an acceptable solution for both you and your customer.

End the call professionally.   As always, be positive and express appreciation for the call.

■ CUSTOMER SERVICE TIPS

What are some things you can do to promote effective customer service? The following tips apply whether you are working with customer service outside your business or within your business.

1. **Follow up with all customers on a regular basis.** Follow-up may be by phone surveys or written surveys.

2. **Treat your customers by using the personal touch.** When you converse with your customers by phone, indicate your willingness to listen to their needs anytime. Write letters or short e-mail messages to them that thank them for their business.

3. **Add your customers' names to mailing lists for publications or newsletters that your company publishes, if there are any.** Customers who have received quality customer service generally like to learn of new products and services, updates, and changes occurring within your company.

4. **Reward and recognize customers for their business and interest.** For example, if a customer refers a possible new customer to your company, let the customer know you appreciate the referral. You can show your appreciation by writing or calling the customer.

5. **Offer special discounts or other similar programs to promote goodwill with your customers.** You will reward your customers for their past business and increase the chances for future business.

6. **Provide standards of excellence for all employees who deal with customers.** Procedures for managing certain customer service requests and concerns should be established and understood by all customer service representatives. These standards and expectations indicate that your business is committed to top customer service performance.

7. **Ask for suggestions from all customers.** The best ideas for improvement often come from customers. Get their input regularly.

8. **Be willing to negotiate possible solutions that will keep everyone satisfied.** This willingness will lead to increased customer satisfaction.

9. **Recognize that problems will occur with products and service.** Be ready to work through them in a positive manner when they arise.

10. **Know your customers so that you will be able to offer the best possible service to them.** Become familiar with customers' preferences, dislikes, and product or service goals. They will remember your concern and kindness.

SUMMARY

1. Positive customer service is important in establishing goodwill in any business. The lack of positive customer service can result in loss of clients and business, sometimes permanently.

2. Everyone with whom you come in contact is a potential customer. Provide services that will meet the customers' needs positively and invite them to continue doing business with you.

3. You must provide quality customer service in order to keep your customers.

4. When you talk on the phone, your voice is very important in providing and receiving quality customer service.

5. Your voice is what the recipient "hears." Remember to smile when talking on the phone. It makes your voice sound pleasant.

6. Special challenges can be presented when you want to reach a specific person in a customer service call.

7. Answer the phone on the first or second ring. If the phone continues to ring, the caller will not appreciate your lateness and could feel neglected.

8. Active listening is important to communicating effectively with customers.

9. Ask the right questions to carry out customer service effectively.

10. Answering devices, such as voice mail, answering machines, and pagers, are important in phone technology today.

11. Customer service professionals recognize that placing a message on voice mail or an answering machine can create a gap between them and their customers. Because of this gap, the possibility exists that the customer and the professional may never be in touch with each other again.

12. Expert customer service centers around questions. The questions should help you provide service for your customers with a personal, helpful style.

13. Answering devices can increase productivity and serve customers better if customer service representatives return calls to customers who have left messages.

14. Pagers, or beepers, can improve customer service because they instantly notify the user of a call. This is especially important when the user is unreachable by phone.

15. The Internet, e-mail, and the World Wide Web are being used more and more to purchase many products and services. These technologies also are being used to report and respond to customer service needs.

16. When a customer raises an objection, you must handle the situation quickly and effectively.

17. Listening is the key to managing objections.

APPLICATION ACTIVITY 5-1

Your Perception of Customer Service

Directions: *On the lines provided below, list several major reasons why customers might want to discontinue doing business with a company. Then, for each of these reasons, write suggestions for correcting the poor customer service. Be specific and ready to justify your answers.*

Reasons for Discontinuing Business	Suggestions for Correcting Poor Customer Service
1.	
2.	
3.	
4.	
5.	
6.	
7.	
8.	
9.	
10.	

APPLICATION ACTIVITY 5-2

Customer Service Courtesy

Directions: *Write answers to the following situations demonstrating positive customer courtesy. Frame your questions to obtain the necessary information in a courteous manner.*

1. Your customer has told you how to get to their home. You only have been able to catch part of the directions. How would you ask your customer to repeat the information?

   _____

   _____

2. You were interrupted by a colleague when attempting to key in the problem on your computer a customer is telling you via the phone. What further questions should you ask?

   _____

   _____

3. You need to follow up with a customer on a specific detail concerning the delivery date. You have two dates listed, and you can't remember which one is preferred. What questions would you ask the customer after you make the call?

   _____

   _____

4. You completely missed the last comment an irate customer made to you because you got distracted by a colleague bringing you lunch. This call is extremely important—you must gain control of yourself quickly. What would you say to your customer?

   _____

   _____

CASE STUDY 5.1

Assessing Customer Service

Directions: *Analyze the situation described below and then answer the questions that follow. Try to provide answers that reflect your understanding of the concepts presented in Chapter 5.*

Clothing Unlimited Company is very successful. You have recently accepted a position as the customer service manager and are anxious to keep the reputation of the company at a high level. In order to gather feedback from customers, you decide to conduct a phone survey to 100 customers over the next two months.
   The survey yields this interesting information:

- 55 percent rated customer service as "average"
- 25 percent rated customer service as "poor"
- 15 percent rated customer service as "good"
- 5 percent rated customer service as "outstanding"

1. Does the fact that only 5 percent indicated customer service was outstanding mean anything? If so, what?

   _____

   _____

   _____

   _____

   _____

   _____

2. What do you feel will happen to Clothing Unlimited Company if this situation is not corrected?

   _____

   _____

   _____

   _____

   _____

3. List at least three major considerations that Clothing Unlimited Company should consider implementing in order to upgrade its overall customer service.

   _____

   _____

   _____

   _____

   _____

4. Do you feel this phone survey was effective? Why or why not?

_____

_____

_____

_____

_____

5. What unique factors might be considered in a phone survey conducted about Clothing Unlimited Company?

_____

_____

_____

_____

_____

CASE STUDY 5.2

Your Attitude Controls Your Altitude

Sheri was excited! She had been working for the Morgan Antique Company for nearly a year. During that time a large part of her job involved handling sales online and using the phone. Today she began a new position with the company that involved taking customer service calls concerning a new line of antiques—costume jewelry. She loved jewelry and had studied this particular line before agreeing to this new assignment. Additionally, Sheri would be receiving a commission on every piece of jewelry she sold.

The day got off to a bad start when she overslept and then got caught in traffic. When she finally got to work a half hour late, her boss made a remark concerning her lateness and had placed another employee at her station. Sheri was annoyed as she had never been late before. Sheri was prepared to service customers, sell product, and enjoy the first day in her new position—and now this!

What should she do?

Directions: *Write a possible solution supported by your phone skill knowledge.*

_____

_____

_____

_____

_____

_____

Using Phone and Phone-Related Equipment and Technology

"What would life be if we had no courage to attempt anything?"
—Vincent Van Gogh

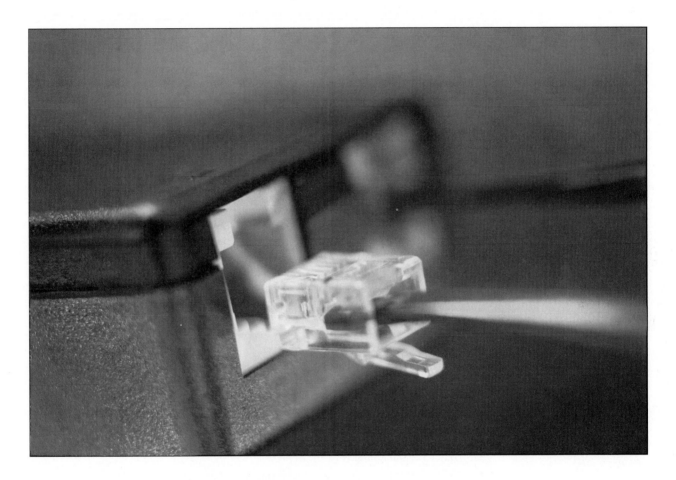

CHAPTER OBJECTIVES

Chapter 6 will help you:

1. Learn and apply efficient use of phone and phone-related equipment and technology in the communication process.

2. Assess phones and phone-related equipment and technology in order to make knowledgeable decisions concerning their use and application.

3. Integrate phone equipment and phone-related technology for maximum use.

■ TODAY'S PHONE TECHNOLOGY

When Alexander Graham Bell experimented and invented the first phone in 1876, phone technology centered around experimenting with equipment needed to "connect" between phones. Today's diversified and sophisticated phone technology provides us with many choices of equipment as an outgrowth of Bell's early research, and phone technology used properly provides instant access to communicating globally.

Phone and/or Phone System Selection

Selecting a phone is an extremely important decision and should not be made lightly. Wireless flexibility is providing options that are eliminating barriers that formerly were created by location. In most cases, you will need to do extensive research before you select a phone and/or phone system.

Keep the following points in mind when making a phone selection:

- What is the size of your business?
- What are your individual needs?
- What is your budget?
- What features do you need? (Among the most common features you would probably want to consider would be call waiting, speed dialing, voice mail, call forwarding, hold, and providing for the disabled.)
- What other phone-related equipment do you need to consider?
- Will your phone and/or phone system be easy to upgrade?
- Should you consider purchasing, renting, or leasing?
- Will you need to consider having a speakerphone or videoconferencing capabilities?
- Should you consider a toll-free number option for incoming calls?
- Are there additional automated features you should consider?

FIGURE 6.1 |

Phones Are Available with Various Styles, Options, and Features.

Cordless (Portable) Phones

Cordless (also often called portable) phones operate by using a transmitter and receiver in both the headset and the base. These types of phones are extremely popular because of their portability, ease of use, and inclusion of many features. In order to function properly, the base of the phone must be connected to a phone line and plugged into an electrical outlet. Headsets of cordless phones use batteries. Cordless phones, while portable, work only within a certain range that is determined by the model selected. Cordless phones come in a wide variety of styles, colors, and prices based primarily on individual needs.

FIGURE 6.2 | Cordless Phones Are Portable and Are Available with Various Styles and Features.

Cell Phones

Cell phones are portable phones that operate wirelessly using "cells" inside the phone that divide the service areas into base stations known as "cells." You might say that a cell phone is a form of a two-way radio with sophisticated services. As you travel with a cell phone, calls you make are routed from station to station, which makes communication seamless as long as you have selected a plan that provides coverage for the area from which you are calling. Companies abound that are carriers of cell phone service plans.

Cell phones were actually outgrowths of headset technology introduced by Dr. Martin Cooper. Dr. Cooper worked for Motorola at the time and made

FIGURE 6.3 I Cell Phones Can Be Used Virtually Anywhere.

the first call on a cell phone to a colleague who worked in research at Bell Laboratories in 1973. It is interesting to note that cell phone technology was introduced in 1947 as part of improved communication in police car technology. From 1947 to 1982 research continued on transmission options and many of the other intricate details involved in determining a feasible and efficient cell phone transmission and service plan. It was not until 1982 that the United States was approved for commercial cell phone service by the Federal Communications Commission. From that point forward, cell phone use has escalated to phenomenal heights and continues as ongoing evolving phone technology by providing a sense of security and access in the process of communication.

Considerations When Purchasing a Cell Phone

Keep the following points in mind if you are considering purchasing a cell phone:

Consider the service plan very carefully to be sure it matches your needs. Service plans come basically in "prepaid" and "monthly." A prepaid plan allows you to spread your cost over several months and would probably work best if you do not use your cell phone often. Otherwise, using a monthly plan would work better in that you will be paying a flat fee monthly. In either case, be certain that you study the plans for possible "extra" charges that you might not be aware of initially.

Consider whether you will want to keep your regular "land-line" (home) number if you have one or whether you will want to go totally wireless and have your phone number go directly to your cell phone. If you choose a cell phone, you will have immediate access to your messages and calls. You also can have a home number that you as well as others are very familiar with transferred to become your cell phone number. The down side of totally using a cell phone is that it could be costly if you are not thoroughly familiar with the service plan. Also, reception and service could be a problem—and a major problem if you needed to dial 911 in an emergency.

Consider your Internet access needs. There are cell phones available that will allow you to access the Internet. When considering this option, you will need to carefully consider the cost as well as how often you would be accessing the Internet.

Consider purchasing options carefully. When you purchase a cell phone, the physical piece of equipment is usually tied to the service. Cell phones come in all sizes, shapes, and colors with a wide variety of configurations. You can purchase a cell phone independently before you go to a service provider, but you need to be aware that some of the services may be unique to the provider. Know what you want for options on your cell phone initially. From there, you can research cell phones extensively before you purchase. Talking to others who are thoroughly familiar with cell phones is helpful and can save you time. In all cases, shop around carefully.

Phone Equipment for Those with Special Needs

Today's population includes many people with special needs that can be barriers to using the phone and phone technology effectively. The level of special needs varies with the individual. Some special needs arise through the aging process, and others arise through accidents or other disabling physical problems. Whatever the special need, phone equipment and technology should be carefully considered to be sure individuals have access to the phone that will help them to communicate in a clear and effective manner.

To aid the person with impaired vision or vision loss, phones are available with special features for the keypad. These features include oversized numbers, enlarged touch-tone keypad, and raised touch-tone keypad. Bright-colored stickers of enlarged numbers printed in dark colors such as black or dark blue may be placed on the keypad of regular touch-tone phones.

Raised and enlarged touch-tone keypads can assist the user who is experiencing motion loss or impairment in pressing the correct buttons. Overlays for keypads are also available that can automatically dial the operator when they are pressed, and a device is available that enables a breath of air to place, receive, and disconnect calls.

For those with hearing and speech impairments, services are available through TRS (Telecommunications Relay Service) to communicate efficiently using a text-based format to key messages. In order to utilize this service, you will need to check with your local service provider to identify the process and procedure to work with your phone. Individuals with speech impairment may use an artificial larynx (voice box) to produce sounds for speaking on the phone. Fax machines may also be used to send and receive messages as well as e-mail and other online communication services.

Auxiliary Phone Equipment

Auxiliary phone equipment is used to support and enhance the process of communication and includes answering and fax machines.

Answering machines are available with many configurations and features. Most answering machines are built in phones today, but they are also available as stand-alone machines, depending on individual preference.

FIGURE 6.4 | Some Answering Machines Use a Tape to Record Messages; Some Record Messages Digitally.

Fax machines can electronically read, send, and receive characters and graphics transmitted over a phone line. A phone can be a part of, or connected to, a fax machine and needs a phone line in order to send and receive faxes. The line may be the regular phone line or a separate phone line designated for the fax machine. Consider these advantages of having a designated line for faxing:

- The line will always be available for immediate use.
- Messages can be received and transmitted 24 hours a day.
- Use of the phone will not interfere with use of the fax machine.

FIGURE 6.5 | Fax Machines Receive Documents on Either Plain Paper or Thermal Paper.

When a message is sent using a fax machine, the operator inserts a document into the fax machine feed tray. The operator then punches in the destination fax number. When the phone connection is made between the two machines, the sending fax machine scans and sends the inserted document, which includes text and graphics. At the destination fax machine, the call is answered, and the message is printed on paper.

The speed of the transmission varies, depending on the density of the text in the document being sent and the individual fax machine. Usually several pages may be sent each minute. The clarity of a faxed document containing text and graphics will be slightly less than that of the original document.

Consider these factors when purchasing a fax machine:

- **Cost and quality of the transmission.** Fax machines receive messages on plain paper and thermal paper, with plain paper usually being the preference because of the quality.

- **Options.** Major options include copying capabilities, redial, adjustments for contrast and resolution, and memory. Study the literature from fax machine manufacturers to assist you in choosing the right machine for your needs.

Modems

Modem is a short term for modulator/demodulator. A modem is an electronic device used to send data from one computer to another across phone lines. The device converts electronic data and images from a sending computer into signals for the receiving computer. The receiving computer, in turn, converts the signals into a form that it can understand. Modems are available as separate devices; however, they are more commonly built into computers.

Consider these points when selecting a modem.

1. **Speed.** A modem's speed is measured by its baud rate. The baud rate is the speed at which the modem converts signals. The higher the baud rate, the faster the modem operates.

2. **Compatibility.** Select a modem that supports software you are using.

FIGURE 6.6 | A Modem Enables Data to Be Transmitted between Computers across Phone Lines.

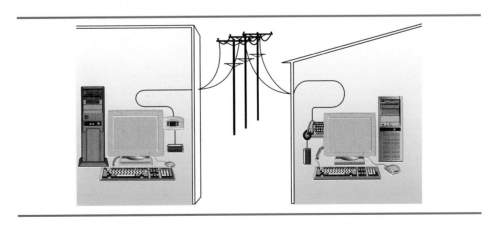

Keep These Fax Tips in Mind

Include a fax cover sheet, or transmittal sheet. (See the example shown in Figure 6.7.)

A fax cover sheet should contain these items:

- Date
- Sender's name
- Sender's company name and address
- Sender's phone number
- Sender's fax number
- Sender's e-mail address, if available
- Number of pages being sent
- Recipient's name
- Recipient's company name
- Recipient's fax number
- Space for a brief transmittal message

Preprinted fax cover sheets are available at most office supply centers.

Limit fax transmissions to as few pages as possible. If you have numerous pages to send, consider sending them by another method, such as overnight delivery or mail. Be concise in fax documents.

Use fonts (typefaces) in your document that are easily readable. Most fax machines receive documents in reduced size, so choose fonts carefully. Use simple, plain fonts, rather than decorative or elaborate fonts (e.g., wide, thick, or script characters). Also, use 12 point size or larger fonts. Avoid using numerous fonts, which can confuse the reader and distract from the message.

FIGURE 6.7 | A Fax Cover Sheet.

Kilburn Glassware
24 Maplewood Ave.
Cornish, ME 04020
Phone: 207-555-0987

Date _8/21/04_
Fax To _Dan & Peggy Dearborn_
Company _Wales Glassware_
Fax No _1-207-555-3420_

From _Cecile Kilburn_   Fax _1-207-555-4371_

Subject _Glassware Quote_   No. of Pages _3_

MESSAGE

Dan & Peggy,
Here are the specifications of the cranberry glass pieces
we discussed!
_CK_

Choose a pager with a display that you can easily read.

Pagers

Pagers and beepers are widely used and have several options. Choose a pager that is of a convenient size and is not cumbersome. Check the display to be sure you can easily read it. Purchase a pager with features that you will use; unused features will cost you money. Refer to Chapter 5 for additional information.

ACTIVITY 6-1

Selecting Phones

Purpose: To help you understand the importance of properly assessing and selecting phones.

Directions: *Select two people to interview concerning their preferences on the purchase of phones. Use the questions below as guidelines to begin your conversation. Share your findings with the class.*

1.   How many phones do you use at home and at work?

2.   What were your considerations when you purchased your phone(s)?

3.   Are the phones adequately meeting your needs? If not, why not?

4.   What other types of auxiliary phone equipment and technology might you consider useful for your needs? Why or why not?

5.   What other recommendations do you have for purchasing phones and auxiliary phone equipment?

ACTIVITY 6-2

Using Phone-Related Equipment

Purpose: To help you properly assess auxiliary phone equipment.

Directions: *The person described in each scenario below is using auxiliary phone equipment in order to be more efficient. Read each statement and then indicate the equipment that applies best, choosing from the letters* **"a"** *through* **"e"** *for your responses.*

       a. Answering machine

       b. Voice Mail

       c. Pager

       d. Computer

       e. Fax machine

_____   1.   When Kenneth Dearborn arrived at work this morning, he noticed the red light flashing on his phone, indicating that he had messages.

_____   2.   Rebecca Wong used this device to transmit electronic data from her company's computer to her client's computer.

_____   3.   Jessica Jones called her office when this device sounded a tone.

———   **4.** Emily Bruciamann needs to send a two-page schedule concerning upcoming meetings to another colleague in her state.

———   **5.** Michael Borden called a company to speak with a sales associate concerning a special order. The sales associate is not in but would like to have Joshua leave a message.

■ ONLINE TECHNOLOGY

Online technology uses computers, phone lines, and other electronic devices to transmit and receive data. Online technology is constantly changing to meet the needs of its users and will continue to do so as communication serves the global marketplace. Online services most frequently used include electronic mail (e-mail) and the Internet.

Electronic Mail (E-Mail)

Electronic mail (also referred to as **e-mail**) is a means of sharing information or communicating between users by way of electronic messages.

Electronic mail (e-mail) is one of the most popular forms of communication and may be provided directly through an Internet service provider or through your own local service provider. Once you have an e-mail account set up, you have instant access to anyone else who has an e-mail address that you know and wish to communicate with. Connection is done via a phone line or a high-speed power line. Prices vary, so it is important to shop around for the best buy that meets your needs.

An e-mail address may contain an abbreviated part of a company or individual's name, an abbreviated part of the online service provider's name, and other parts, known as subdomains and domains. For example, an e-mail address might read:

edrinkwater@painterstown.com

edrinkwater@fed.gov

edrinkwater@education.adelphia.net

Major advantages of using e-mail are:

- **It can save money.** Messages can be written off-line before they are sent online.

- **It can be sent at your convenience.** Time zone differences do not affect sending e-mail messages.

- **It can be read at your convenience.** You can eliminate phone tag and save time by avoiding repeat calls.

- **It can notify the sender that a recipient has opened an e-mail message.** You can eliminate placing repeat calls and leaving messages.

E-mail is similar to regular mail in several ways. You must open your e-mail as with a letter in an envelope. If you open it, though, you do not necessarily have to read it. Some software e-mail programs provide an opportunity for you to click on a section of the software where you can note whether the e-mail you sent has been read as well as the time it was read. This helps greatly in determining what is happening with the e-mail you sent, especially if you are waiting for a reply.

Be prepared to follow up e-mail messages that are not answered within a reasonable amount of time. You may want to phone or send another message to that person.

Another very important e-mail feature is sending a separate page of information known as an "attachment." An attachment is a separate file that is attached to your e-mail electronically. You do need to remember to limit the size of your attachment as it can create transmission problems on occasion. Also, you need to be extremely careful with attachments accompanying e-mails as that is where viruses are located. If you open an attachment that has a virus, major problems can arise including the possibility of ruining your hard drive with all your stored data. An important point to keep in mind is to be sure to use a virus protection software program on your computer system. By doing this, you can often prevent major catastrophes from occurring.

Managing E-Mail Messages

Use these guidelines to help you manage your e-mail professionally.

Check your e-mail daily.   Messages can be sent anytime. Check periodically to avoid missing important messages. Some messages may require timely action or follow up.

Delete unnecessary messages; save important ones.   After you have read your e-mail, delete messages that need no reply. Keep messages that you must respond to or follow up.

Be aware that e-mail can be monitored.   Some businesses monitor e-mail for security reasons. Be careful what you send and to whom you send it.

Be professional in all e-mail correspondence.   Use the same courtesies as you would if the message were in hard copy, such as a letter or memo.

Be concise.   Avoid using unnecessary words. Keep your message brief.

Use a memo format for messages.   It is not necessary to format an e-mail message in a letter format—the simpler the better.

Avoid shouting.   E-mail users should respect e-mail etiquette. The use of all-capital letters in messages is considered equal to verbally shouting. The use of all-capital letters can dilute the real message.

Proofread messages before sending them.   As with all correspondence, review and proofread e-mail messages before sending them.

The Internet

The *Internet* is a worldwide collection of computer networks providing connectivity via phone lines, satellites, wireless connections, fiber optic lines, and coaxial cables. Sources of information are available through individual Web pages, commercial Web pages, libraries, and other information sources simply by clicking on to an Internet service provider. Once connected, it is important for you to know the exact address such as www.edrinkwater.com. If you do not know the exact address or if you are searching for specific information, you will need to use one of the many search engines that can direct you to many topics. A search engine is an electronic method of researching. There are many, many search engines available for research. Most search engines specialize in particular topics and ways of searching. Several search engines include many other search engines within theirs. Learning to use a search engine efficiently takes practice and patience as well as developing the knowledge of determining exactly what you are searching for as well as which search engine is best to use for the search. To do this, you will need to enter one or two identifying words for purposes of searching. You can waste a great deal of time and effort searching aimlessly in cyberspace if you are not careful. Unless you are simply "searching for fun," you need to become familiar with the most reliable search engines.

Connection to the Internet is usually accomplished by one of the following ways:

- Using an Internet service provider (ISP) and using a modem.
- Using a digital subscriber line (DSL).
- Using the computer attached to its own network at work.
- Using a wireless connection.

Selecting an Internet provider depends on what your needs are as they relate to both your personal and professional requirements. Keep these important points in mind when using the Internet:

- Know the exact address if possible. This will save you a lot of time.
- Be sure that you are using a secure server.
- Use virus software to protect your system.
- Do not give out personal information such as your credit card number or Social Security number on a site that you feel is not secure.

ACTIVITY 6-3

Choosing Auxiliary Phone Equipment and Tools

Purpose: The purpose of this activity is to learn to properly assess and choose between auxiliary phone equipment and tools.

Directions: *Read each scenario below. Then indicate which auxiliary phone device(s) or tools would best suit each situation. Be prepared to justify your answer.*

1. You need to send a one-page letter instead of making a phone call.

   _____

2. You are in the attic searching for tax records in preparation for going to your accountant. You want to be able to answer any calls.

   _____

3. You are traveling 350 miles on business and want to have a phone available for your use during your travel.

   _____

4. You will be away from your desk for two days but wish to receive all your calls.

_____

5. You want to be able to receive any messages immediately wherever you are.

_____

6. You would like to be able to do some shopping in the convenience of your home via a computer.

_____

7. You want to be able to communicate electronically with your staff located at ten places in the United States.

_____

SUMMARY

1. Alexander Graham Bell's research and work led to the invention of the phone in 1876. For some time after, phone technology focused on developing equipment because of the need to make connections between phones. The progress in phone and phone-related equipment and technology today is an outgrowth of this work.

2. Phone equipment that is properly installed provides access to instant communication globally.

3. The need for phones and phone-related equipment should be a high priority for you and your company.

4. Evaluate a phone system carefully. Be sure it will adequately serve your customers, potential customers, co-workers, and everyone with whom you do business.

5. When choosing phone equipment, think what will best meet your needs, whether you buy one phone or many.

6. Cordless phones are popular because they are portable and available in many styles and features.

7. Cell phones can be used anywhere where there is a signal.

8. Many phone and phone-related equipment products are available to provide for those with special needs.

9. A modem is an electronic device used to send data from one computer to another across phone lines.

10. A fax machine can electronically read, send, and receive characters and most forms of illustration transmitted over a phone line.

11. Pagers and beepers are widely used and come equipped with a variety of options.

12. Online technology uses computers and phone lines or electronic devices to transmit and receive data. This technology already provides many products and services to individuals and businesses including e-mail and Internet.

APPLICATION ACTIVITY 6–1

Recommending Phone and Auxiliary Equipment

Directions: _Assume that Natasha Winslow is opening her own small business, where she will manage all the calls. On the lines provided below, write a statement recommending the type of phone and auxiliary phone equipment Natasha should purchase. Base your recommendations on what you have_ *studied in Chapter 6. Report this information to your classmates or as your instructor directs you.*

_____

_____

_____

_____

_____

_____

_____

_____

_____

_____

_____

_____

_____

APPLICATION ACTIVITY 6-2

Shopping for a Cell Phone

Purpose: To give you insight into considering your priorities when shopping for a cell phone.

Directions: *Place a check mark beside the statement as it applies. When you mark a statement "maybe," be prepared to justify why you are questioning the statement.*

		Yes	No	Maybe
1.	Is battery life important?	_____	_____	_____
2.	Are color and weight important?	_____	_____	_____
3.	Should I use a prepaid plan?	_____	_____	_____
4.	Should I have to pay for the phone?	_____	_____	_____
5.	Is Web browsing important to me?	_____	_____	_____
6.	Should I be able to use the cell phone as a pager?	_____	_____	_____
7.	Do I want voice mail capability?	_____	_____	_____
8.	Do I need caller ID?	_____	_____	_____
9.	Can the cell phone hold an address book of frequently used numbers?	_____	_____	_____
10.	Do I want call waiting?	_____	_____	_____

Analysis: Have a conversation with a partner to see what your priorities were? What have you learned from doing this activity?

APPLICATION ACTIVITY 6-3

How Should I Behave with My Cell Phone?

Purpose: To develop an awareness of proper use of cell phones.

Directions: *Read the statements below and check "Acceptable" or "Unacceptable." If a statement is "Unacceptable," be prepared to explain why.*

	Acceptable	Unacceptable
1. Because it is church, it is fine to leave your cell phone on.	_____	_____
2. It's a good idea not to have long conversations on a cell phone.	_____	_____
3. If you have a good driving record, it's fine to make a call on a cell phone while driving.	_____	_____
4. When in a group, it is preferred to ask if it's all right to use a cell phone.	_____	_____
5. It's best to turn off your cell phone when you are in a restaurant.	_____	_____

Analysis: Discuss your choices with a partner.

Answer the question below.

What are your biggest concerns when it comes to using a cell phone?

_____

_____

_____

_____

_____

What steps will you take to ensure that your cell phone etiquette is the best possible?

_____

_____

_____

_____

CASE STUDY 6.1

The Home Insurance Adjuster

Directions: *Analyze the situation described below and then answer the questions that follow. Try to provide answers that reflect your understanding of the concepts presented in Chapter 6.*

Cherise Nguben is an insurance adjuster for a large insurance company that processes claims electronically. In her job, Cherise uses the phone continuously. She also receives calls from claims adjusters in the field, who are difficult to reach because they frequently travel. Cherise uses e-mail and her fax machine to send documents and data electronically in communicating with co-workers (both in her building and at other branch offices) and clients.

The company has agreed to Cherise's request to work out of her home. In order to facilitate her work, the company will provide for Cherise a computer and any necessary auxiliary phone equipment.

1. What type of phone would best serve Cherise's needs? Why?

_____

_____

_____

_____

2. Would a cordless phone or a cellular phone be useful to Cherise? Why or why not?

_____

_____

_____

_____

3. What auxiliary phone equipment will Cherise need? Why?

_____

_____

_____

_____

4. What additional phone services, features, or equipment would be useful to Cherise for:

a. Ensuring that she misses no calls?

_____

_____

_____

_____